Base Development 1965-1970

Base Development
in
South Vietnam

1965-1970

By

Lieutenant General Carroll H. Dunn

GOVERNMENT REPRINTS PRESS
Washington, D.C.

© Ross & Perry, Inc. 2002 on new material. All rights reserved.

No claim to U.S. government work contained throughout this book.

Protected under the Berne Convention.

Printed in The United States of America
Ross & Perry, Inc. Publishers
216 G St., N.E.
Washington, D.C. 20002
Telephone (202) 675-8300
Facsimile (801)459-7535
info@RossPerry.com

SAN 253-8555

Government Reprints Press Edition 2002

Government Reprints Press is an Imprint of Ross & Perry, Inc.

Library of Congress Control Number: 2001097206
http://www.GPOreprints.com

ISBN 1-931839-32-8

Book Cover designed by Sapna. sapna@rossperry.com

☻ The paper used in this publication meets the requirements for permanence established by the American National Standard for Information Sciences "Permanence of Paper for Printed Library Materials" (ANSI Z39.48-1984).

All rights reserved. No copyrighted part of this publication may be reproduced, stored in a retrieval system, or transmitted, in any form or by any means, electronic, photocopying, recording, or otherwise, without the prior written permission of the publisher.

Base Development
in
South Vietnam

1965-1970

By

Lieutenant General Carroll H. Dunn

GOVERNMENT REPRINTS PRESS
Washington, D.C.

© Ross & Perry, Inc. 2002 on new material. All rights reserved.

No claim to U.S. government work contained throughout this book.

Protected under the Berne Convention.

Printed in The United States of America
Ross & Perry, Inc. Publishers
216 G St., N.E.
Washington, D.C. 20002
Telephone (202) 675-8300
Facsimile (801)459-7535
info@RossPerry.com

SAN 253-8555

Government Reprints Press Edition 2002

Government Reprints Press is an Imprint of Ross & Perry, Inc.

Library of Congress Control Number: 2001097206
http://www.GPOreprints.com

ISBN 1-931839-32-8

Book Cover designed by Sapna. sapna@rossperry.com

⊗ The paper used in this publication meets the requirements for permanence established by the American National Standard for Information Sciences "Permanence of Paper for Printed Library Materials" (ANSI Z39.48-1984).

All rights reserved. No copyrighted part of this publication may be reproduced, stored in a retrieval system, or transmitted, in any form or by any means, electronic, photocopying, recording, or otherwise, without the prior written permission of the publisher.

Foreword

The United States Army has met an unusually complex challenge in Southeast Asia. In conjunction with the other services, the Army has fought in support of a national policy of assisting an emerging nation to develop governmental processes of its own choosing, free of outside coercion. In addition to the usual problems of waging armed conflict, the assignment in Southeast Asia has required superimposing the immensely sophisticated tasks of a modern army upon an underdeveloped environment and adapting them to demands covering a wide spectrum. These involved helping to fulfill the basic needs of an agrarian population, dealing with the frustrations of antiguerrilla operations, and conducting conventional campaigns against well-trained and determined regular units.

As this assignment nears an end, the U.S. Army must prepare for other challenges that may lie ahead. While cognizant that history never repeats itself exactly and that no army ever profited from trying to meet a new challenge in terms of the old one, the Army nevertheless stands to benefit immensely from a study of its experience, its shortcomings no less than its achievements.

Aware that some years must elapse before the official histories will provide a detailed and objective analysis of the experience in Southeast Asia, we have sought a forum whereby some of the more salient aspects of that experience can be made available now. At the request of the Chief of Staff, a representative group of senior officers who served in important posts in Vietnam and who still carry a heavy burden of day-to-day responsibilities has prepared a series of monographs. These studies should be of great value in helping the Army develop future operational concepts while at the same time contributing to the historical record and providing the American public with an interim report on the performance of men and officers who have responded, as others have through our history, to exacting and trying demands.

All monographs in the series are based primarily on official records, with additional material from published and unpublished secondary works, from debriefing reports and interviews with key participants, and from the personal experience of the author. To facilitate security clearance, annotation and detailed bibliography have been omitted from the published version; a fully documented account with bibliography is filed with the Office of the Chief of Military History.

Lieutenant General Carroll H. Dunn is specially qualified to tell the story of Base Development construction in Vietnam. A professional engineer since the beginning of his Army career, General Dunn has been the Director of the Army Waterways Experiment Station, Executive Officer to the Chief of Engineers (responsible for the construction of the nation's first ballistic missile warning system), and both Director and Deputy Commander of the Titan II Missile System construction program. As Engineer for the Army's Southwestern Division, he supervised construction of the Manned Spacecraft Center at Houston. In January 1966 he became Director of Construction for the U.S. Military Assistance Command in Vietnam, responsible for all Department of Defense construction in the country. In June 1966 he became Assistant Chief of Staff for Logistics and held that post until his return to the United States in the fall of 1967. He was then assigned as Director of Military Construction, Office of the Chief of Engineers. In 1969 he was appointed Deputy Chief of Engineers and in August 1971, with promotion to the rank of lieutenant general, he became Director of the Defense Nuclear Agency.

Washington, D.C.
30 March 1972

VERNE L. BOWERS
Major General, USA
The Adjutant General

Preface

Before mid-1965, when the first U.S. engineer units arrived, the only American construction capability in Vietnam was a small civilian force under contract to the U.S. Navy. During this period, the Navy's Bureau of Yards and Docks (now the Naval Facilities Engineering Command) and the Army Corps of Engineers shared worldwide responsibility for military construction, with Southeast Asia among the areas assigned to the Navy.

As the military buildup proceeded, engineer and construction forces received high priority for mobilization and deployment. With the coming of contingents of Army engineers, Navy Seabees, Marine Corps engineers, Air Force Prime BEEF and Red Horse units, and civilian contractors, U.S. construction strength in Vietnam increased rapidly. Vietnamese Army engineers and engineer troops of other Free World allies handled some of the construction for their own forces, thereby furthering the over-all effort.

In February 1966 the Directorate of Construction was established in the Military Assistance Command, Vietnam, to provide centralized management of the U.S. program. As the first Director of Construction, I had the duty, as the principal staff officer for engineering and base development, to assure that the construction effort was responsive to tactical needs and priorities. Among my assigned tasks were holding construction to minimum essential requirements and enforcing the most austere standards consistent with operational needs and tactical objectives. Embracing ports, airfields, storage areas, ammunition dumps, housing, bridges, roads, and other conventional facilities, the construction program was probably the largest concentrated effort of its kind in history.

One feature of the program was unique. Because engineer troops were few at the beginning, contractors and civilian workmen for the first time in history assumed a major construction role in an active theater of operations. Without their valuable contribution, many more troops would have been required to do the job.

Formidable obstacles confronted the engineers. The tropical climate, with its monsoon rains and enervating heat, imposed severe handicaps on constructors. Few building materials, either natural or manufactured, were available locally. Saigon was the only deep-draft port. Roads, mostly primitive, were interdicted by the enemy.

Cargoes had to move in coastal vessels or by air. The supply line to the United States stretched ten thousand miles. Native labor was largely unskilled. Because much of the country was thickly populated and graves of venerated ancestors abounded, building sites were at a premium. Complicating the entire construction program was the use of essentially peacetime funding methods in a war situation.

As U.S. forces disengage, American engineers will bequeath a rich legacy to the people of South Vietnam. Much of the construction completed for our forces will serve as a foundation for national development in the years ahead. Seven deep-draft ports exist where there was only one. Similarly, roads, bridges, utilities, and many airfields and other facilities will remain as valuable assets to the country. Perhaps the program's greatest impact has been upon the people themselves. Tens of thousands of Vietnamese have had an opportunity to learn American building techniques and many of them have become skilled welders, electricians, plumbers, carpenters, and heavy-equipment operators. Their competence will contribute immeasurably to the goal of economic viability.

Many people have contributed to the preparation of this monograph, to all of whom I am deeply grateful. I am particularly indebted to the following: Major General Daniel A. Raymond, Colonel Robert B. Burlin, Colonel Edward T. Watling, Lieutenant Colonel Gerald E. Boyer, Dr. Kenneth J. Deacon, Mr. Leon Albin, Mr. Charles J. Owen, and Mr. Boris Levine, Office, Chief of Engineers; Lieutenant Colonel Robert J. Wallace and Major James H. Andrews, U.S. Army Engineer Center, Fort Belvoir. Also, I wish to express my gratitude to the Engineer Strategic Studies Group and the Directorate of Real Estate, OCE, for assistance rendered during development of the manuscript and to Major Robert W. Whitehead, Office, Chief of Engineers, who was the project officer for this monograph.

My thanks to the friends and colleagues who read all or parts of this volume in manuscript form and who provided many important corrections and helpful suggestions. These associates of mine cannot, of course, be held responsible for any views or interpretations which I have advanced.

Washington, D.C.
30 March 1972

CARROLL H. DUNN
Lieutenant General, U.S. Army

Contents

Chapter	Page
I. THE SETTING	3
II. ORGANIZING THE ASSISTANCE EFFORT	13
III. REAL ESTATE AND LAND ACQUISITION	29
IV. PLANNING AND THE CONSTRUCTION CONCEPT	37
V. THE BASES	50
VI. FACILITIES CONSTRUCTION	71
VII. FACILITIES ENGINEERING	89
VIII. THE ROAD PROGRAMS	99
IX. CONSTRUCTION LOGISTICS	113
X. LESSONS AND A LEGACY	132
GLOSSARY	149
INDEX	157

Tables

No.		Page
1.	Construction Standards	45
2.	Construction Appropriations	49
3.	Electric Power Distribution	82
4.	POL Capabilities	130
5.	Major Base Camps	136

Charts

1.	Command Structure in the Pacific	14
2.	MACV Command Structure	15
3.	Organization of MACDC, 1968	22
4.	USARV Engineer Organization	24
5.	Manpower	42
6.	Facilities Maintenance Organization	95
7.	MACV Road Cross Sections	101

Maps

No.		Page
1.	Indochina Physiographic Regions	4
2.	Land Lines of Communication, 1954	8
3.	Provinces of South Vietnam	10
4.	Corps Tactical Zones and Support Command Areas of Responsibility	39
5.	Cam Ranh Bay	56
6.	Qui Nhon	58
7.	Seaports	60
8.	Tactical Airfields, RVN, 1968	66
9.	Hospitals	76
10.	Electric Power Distribution	81
11.	POL Facilities	128
12.	Major Base Camps	135
13.	The Greater Saigon Area	144

Illustrations

	Page
Elements of 1st Cavalry Arrive	20
Early Construction at Cam Ranh Bay	51
A DeLong Pier Under Construction	54
First DeLong in Use	57
Two Caribous	64
Quarters Rise at Long Binh	74
Spiderlike Ducts for a MUST	75
Floating Power Plants	79
LARC V	85
BARC	86
Selection of Buildings Under Construction	88
Seabees in I Corps	91
Vietnamese Firefighter	97
Rock-Crushing Operation	104
Rock Drill	105
Sheepsfoot Roller	106
Scrapers Prepare a Right of Way	108
Vietnamese Engineers	110
Vietnamese Construction Workers	116
D-7 Tractor	120
Repair Parts for Nonstandard Equipment	123

	Page
Bladder Fuel Cells	127
Fuel Pipelines	129
Corporal Mung	140
Student Volunteers	142
Newly Trained Army Engineers	146

All illustrations are from Department of the Army files.

BASE DEVELOPMENT IN
SOUTH VIETNAM

CHAPTER I

The Setting

From the eastern seaboard of the United States the journey to the Republic of Vietnam by merchantman takes thirty-four days—nineteen days from the port of San Francisco. The Asian country is bounded on the north by the Democratic Republic of Vietnam, on the east by the South China Sea, on the southwest by the Gulf of Thailand, and on the west by Laos and Cambodia.

The tropical climate of the countryside changes with the seasonal monsoons. At Saigon, the capital, the temperature varies little from an 84-degree average, but the summer monsoon, gathering moisture over the Indian Ocean, brings heavy rainfall to the southern city. From May through October fifty-eight inches of rain may be expected. Farther north near the old imperial city of Hue 116 inches of rain may be expected toward the end of the year as the monsoon moves farther northward and inland across Asia. Typhoons, or tropical cyclones which originate in the Pacific, strike this sector between September and November, bringing heavy rainfall and causing a great deal of damage at Hue and in its neighboring coastal plain.

As the seasons change, the northeast monsoon, which originates in the interior of Asia, sweeps across the expanses of China bringing clear skies and hot dry weather. For a country of Vietnam's size, stretching as it does seven hundred miles along its length and being as narrow as forty miles across the 17th parallel near the Demilitarized Zone, the seasonal differences are dramatic. Summer weather prevails in the modern capital of Saigon from November to mid-March, while winter rains, mists, and tropical storms lash the ancient capital at Hue.

The long coastline, or eastern border, begins in the north at the Demilitarized Zone, established as a result of the 1954 Geneva Accords, which created the two Vietnams from the former French Indochina colony, and extends southwestward in a gradual curve. The coastline consists of vast stretches of sand spotted by irrigated rice paddies. The Annamite Mountains rise within thirty miles of the coast in some places and as far back as seventy miles in others. The land along the coast which is not covered by drifting sand

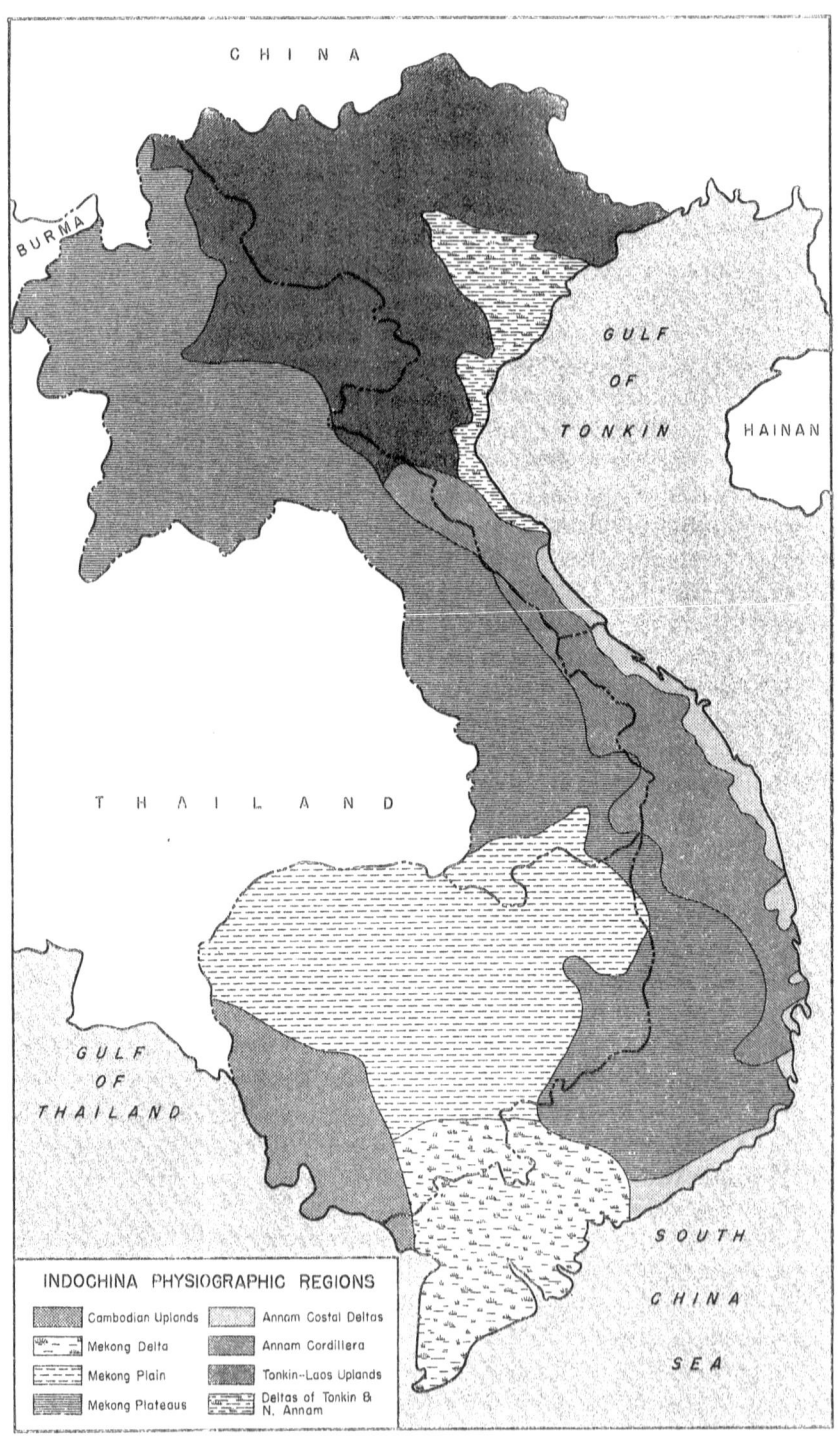

MAP 1

dunes is used for rice farming, although the coastal lands cannot compare with the rich alluvial soil of the delta regions for productivity.

The southernmost third of South Vietnam, the area sometimes known as the delta or the rice basket, was once below sea level and therefore received the rich alluvial deposits of the Mekong River. From prehistoric times the richest soil in Asia has been deposited to form what is now the Ca Mau Peninsula and the Plain of Reeds, or the Mekong and Saigon River Deltas. Some areas in the delta have solidified, while others still remain marshy. The flat muddy coast near the capital is representative of the area's silty clay, which is hundreds of feet deep in places. Alluvial soil constitutes a blessing to the rice grower, but a bane to the builder; when wet it becomes an unmanageable, sticky mass with poor weight-bearing qualities. The region abounds with tributaries and canals of which the French constructed some four thousand kilometers to aid in the transformation of 4.3 million acres of swamp into arable land—a feat surpassing the magnitude of digging for the Suez Canal.

Much as the Mekong rambles to the sea in an apparently aimless wandering, the Annamite Mountains (occasionally called the Annamese Cordillera) are a sometimes rugged, sometimes flattened backbone pressing through much of Indochina and forming the watershed between the Mekong River and the South China Sea. In the north the range extends into North Vietnam, and in the south it becomes the Central Highlands, a plateau area some one hundred miles wide and two hundred miles long, covered, for the most part, with tropical forest. On the east side the range rises steeply from the coastal plains. On the west it gradually descends through a series of plateaus to the level of the Mekong Delta. Because of the steep seaward slopes, the Cordillera forms a partial barrier to inland penetration; and tribes distinct in race and culture from the coastal Vietnamese continue to inhabit the mountains and highlands. (*Map 1*)

The cultural history of the Vietnamese may be traced back to the early Neolithic period. The original inhabitants of Vietnam founded their civilization along the banks and in the delta of the Red River on the Tonkin Gulf very much the way Egyptian civilization developed along the Nile. From the Red River and its rice fields the population expanded. Several centuries of trading with seafaring neighbors, resurgent wars, and invasions gave the people a history deeply interwoven with warfare.

The old kingdom of Annam in what is now the south predates the Second Punic War. Chinese government had taken hold in Vietnam after the successful invasions of the Han dynasty, and

Annam or the "Dominion of the South" was thereafter molded and dominated by the Chinese civilization. Revolts occurred during the period of Chinese colonization which gave the Vietnamese many of their cultural folk heroes and heroines. The country was unified between the eleventh and thirteenth centuries and shortly thereafter repulsed the invasions of Kublai Khan only to fall again to the Chinese in the fifteenth century. With a new dynasty the Vietnamese were again their own masters and proceeded to establish military colonies on the lands of their former masters. By the middle of the sixteenth century the Nguyen family in Hue had firmly established their predominance in the affairs of Annam.

During the sixteenth century contact with the West began. Traders and missionaries arrived to begin a modern era of intrigue. The French made their mark on the people, and with the aid of the church and its lieutenants, the first French-supported emperor gained the Annamese throne early in the nineteenth century. French influence had its ups and downs until the latter half of the nineteenth century when the French made their *de facto* conquest final, but Japanese conquest in World War II upset French rule and resulted in a Vichy government followed by a quasi independence for the Vietnamese. In 1946 the French attempted to reassert their influence in Vietnam, and the resulting war was eventually resolved in the Geneva Accords of 1954. It was during the 1954 Geneva Convention that Vietnam was provisionally divided into two states.

American involvement in the Vietnamese conflict began in the late 1940s with arms aid to the French. Old alliances and the outbreak of the Korean War placed the United States in a political position supporting French colonial policy. In 1955 President Dwight D. Eisenhower, acting under extended provisions of the Southeast Asia Treaty Organization (SEATO) protocol, pledged matériel and advisory assistance to the South Vietnamese. As French Union forces left Vietnam, American military advisory groups assumed the responsibility for training the Vietnamese armed forces. In April 1961 the Kennedy administration signed a Treaty of Amity and Economic Relations declaring its intention to render military aid to the Republic of Vietnam and "preserve its independence." With this resolve, the American military presence in Vietnam increased to four thousand officers and men by the end of 1962.

The economy of Vietnam has suffered to a considerable extent throughout its many years of strife, but rice continues to be the country's principal export. Before World War II only two countries in the world exported more rice than Vietnam, but continued warfare has changed the picture. The exportation of rubber from the huge southern plantations has lost considerable importance since the widespread manufacturing of synthetic rubber, but manioc, sweet potatoes, coconuts, and beans are still exported. The Republic of Vietnam does not have the coal, zinc, tin, chrome, phosphate, or lumber resources of the north. The populace must import most of its heavy equipment and other manufactured goods.

Local markets flourish in South Vietnam. Fish products, pigs, chickens, rice, and small manufactured goods are bought and sold at hamlet and village markets. The village, the second level of governmental hierarchy, still retains the largest proportion of the 17.5 million Vietnamese population. A full 80 percent of the population remains scattered between district capitals and any of the forty-four province capitals with the majority settled in the delta or on the coastal plain between the country's principal railroad line and the main north-south road. Farmers work their crops, and fishermen ply the coastal waterways as do merchants in the small cargo vessels which transport goods between the smaller coastal villages and the major port at Saigon, or the minor ports at Hue or Nha Trang, or the old French naval port at Da Nang.

Few major ports were ever built on the coast, since the economy of the area has never lent itself to full exploitation and shipping has always been exposed to seasonal typhoons and heavy winds during the winter monsoons. Deepwater ports have been entirely unnecessary in Vietnam with the possible exception of Saigon, which sits astride the Saigon River some forty miles inland. The capital, fed by a continuing flow of junks, sampans, river boats, and steamers coming down from upland and out of the Mekong, became the leading port for domestic and foreign trade, since navigation in the delta region had been improved by extended dredging and by canals which cut across swamplands and cultivated fields to join together the many tributaries of the Mekong and Saigon Rivers.

In addition to being South Vietnam's primary seaport, Saigon had also been the country's principal air terminal. As stop-off and refueling points on the international air lanes, Tan Son Nhut and nearby Bien Hoa outside of Saigon were two of Vietnam's three airfields capable of accepting jet aircraft before 1965. Even as late as mid-1966 there were only six airfields capable of landing jet aircraft, and only three of these employed high-intensity lighting. Radio, navigation, and ground equipment were adequate only for existing civilian traffic. The fact that Air Vietnam, the national airline, owned only thirteen aircraft in 1965, none of which were jet powered, is a clue to the paucity of Vietnam's airfield facilities.

The most direct transportation available between major cities

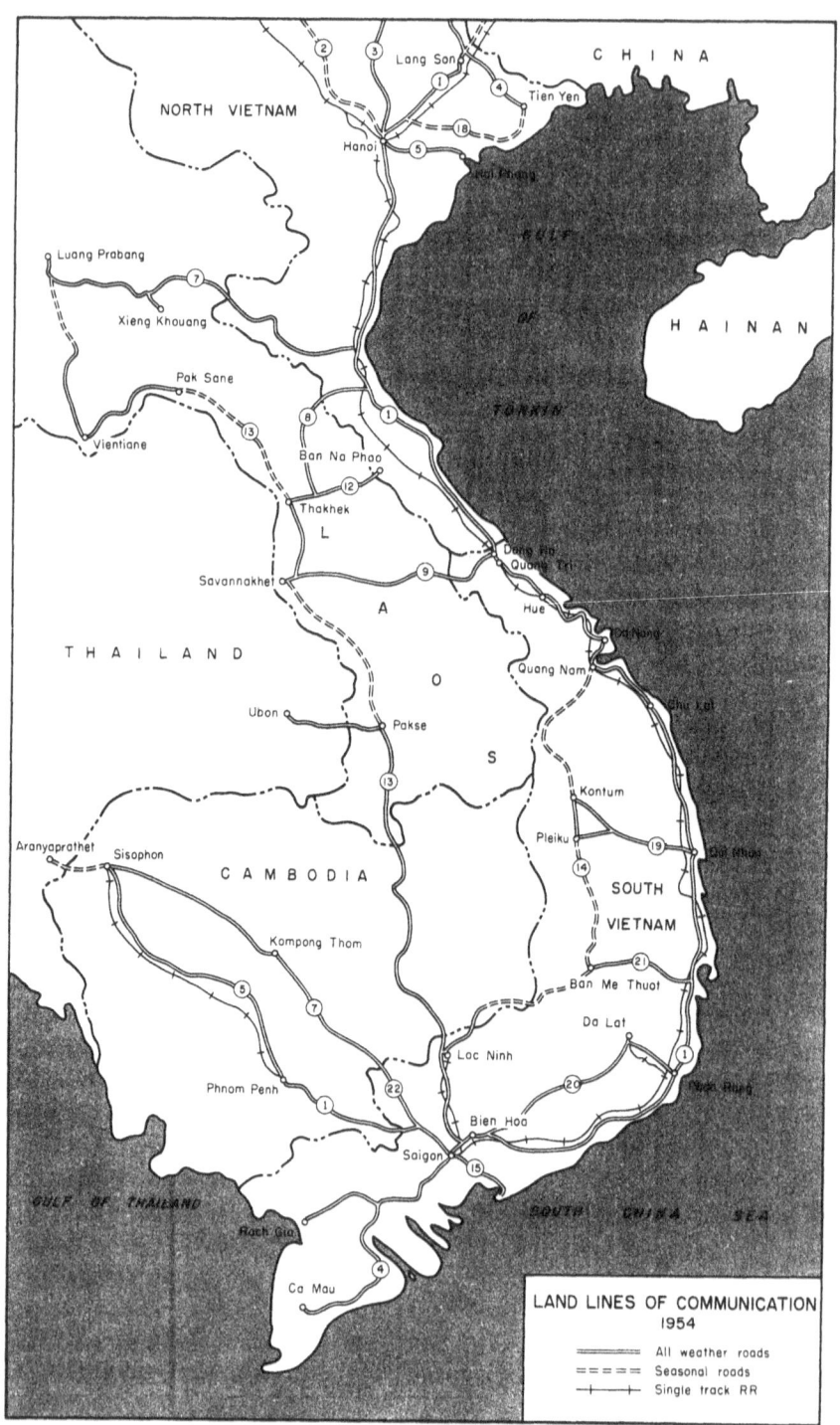

MAP 2

was by rail. The main line of the Vietnamese railroad system, once called the Saigon-Hue-Hanoi Line, was completed in 1936, or fifty-five years after it was begun. The right of way parallels the coast highway, cuts through mountain spurs, and rises over rivers and streams, which lie shallow most of the year but reach flood conditions during the monsoon. The former Trans-Indochina Railroad, which originally comprised some 2,900 kilometers of narrow one-meter gauge track, was the labor of two generations of French and Vietnamese engineers; but for all practical purposes the line ceased to exist after 1965. It was completely destroyed in many places by sabotage or left to fall into disrepair because track security became virtually impossible.

The Vietnamese road system received more attention than the railroad after World War I. (*Map 2*) Main roads were constructed five to six meters wide on level runs, but became narrower as they climbed into the mountains. The vast number of bridges which were required imposed limitations on the builders, although the most frequently constructed bridge was only two and a half to three meters wide. Few roads were asphalted, some were macadamized, but most roads were left unsurfaced. National Route 1, the main north-south coastal highway, was originally very well constructed, since it was the principal national road linking Hanoi in the north with Saigon in the far south. Route 13 was similarly constructed to link Saigon with Cambodia and Laos. Route 14, branching off Route 13, was built through the Central Highlands to join Route 1 again at Da Nang. With secondary roads constructed to link smaller political subdivisions together, the road system became quite adequate for the limited volume and weight of traffic it had to sustain.

The political subdivisions of the countryside from hamlet to village to district and then to province had been satisfactory for civil government, but the return to full-scale military operations and the need for military lines of division and areas of responsibility caused a dividing of the political map into larger military zones. (*Map 3*) Saigon was made into a military district separate and distinct unto itself. The northernmost five provinces became I Corps Tactical Zone. The Central Highlands from Kontum and Binh Dinh Provinces south through Quang Duc, Lam Dong, and Binh Tuy Provinces became II Corps Tactical Zone. III Corps was cut out of the swamps with a southern border of the Song Vam Co Tay, which runs across the narrow southern waist of the republic. The heavily populated delta provinces made up IV Corps Tactical Zone.

With the steady increase in military activity and Vietnam's mobilization for war, the military implications of the Vietnamese setting became matters of prime concern to those who would be

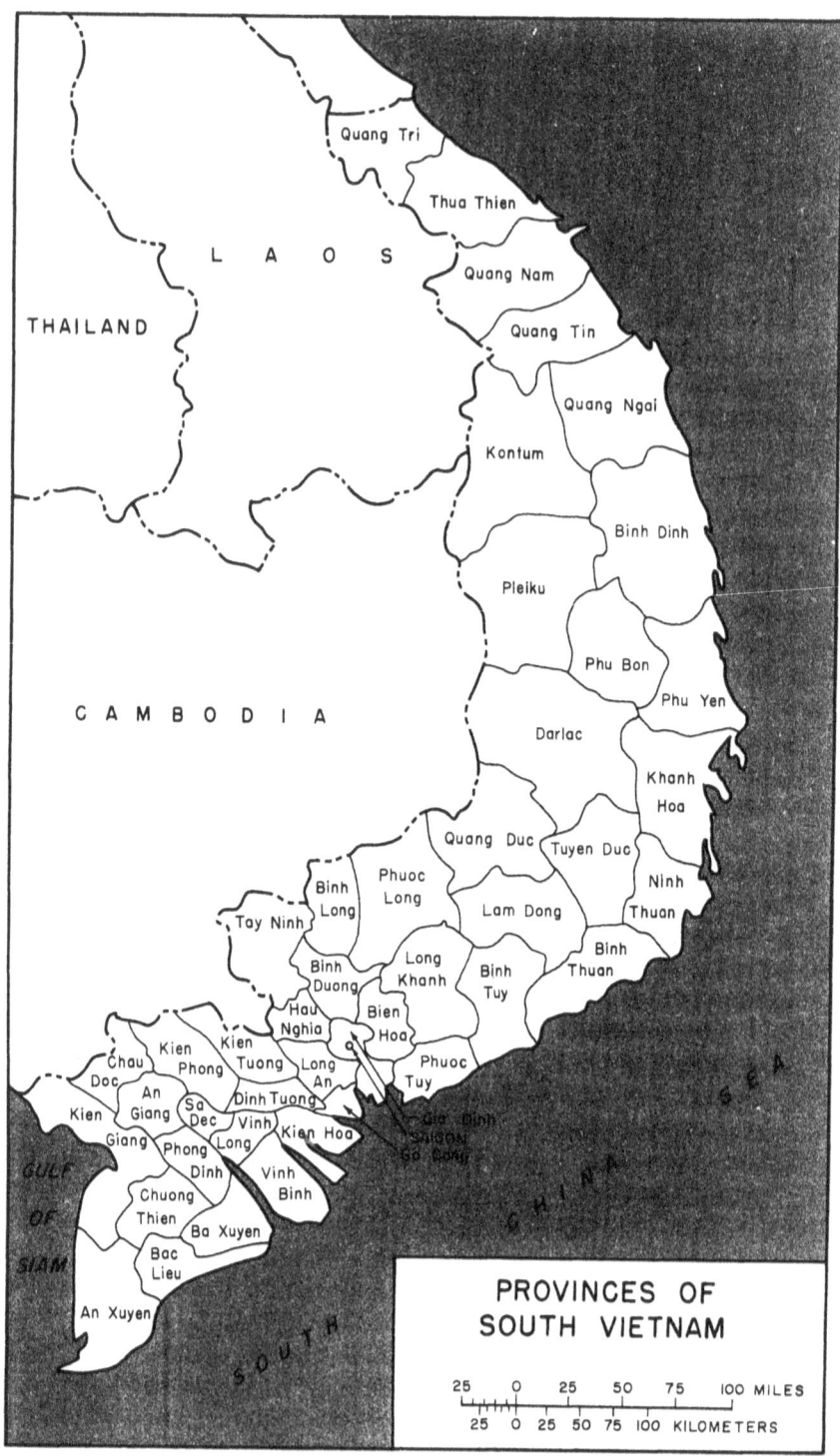

MAP 3

responsible for carrying out tactical operations, providing logistic support, and performing construction. The least significant factors of Vietnamese geography, culture, climate, and habit assumed new dimensions and importance. The simple matter of water supply illustrates the kind of problem which would soon have to be dealt with.

Most of the inhabitants of Vietnam obtain their water from streams, irrigation canals and ditches, or shallow wells, which are often contaminated. In rural areas these sources are used indiscriminately for laundry, watering animals, cooking, and drinking. In the Mekong and Dong Na Deltas, tides cause waterways to become brackish as far inland as sixty miles. Some wells in these areas are drilled to a depth of 500 feet before a desirable stratum is reached. Although the U.S. Agency for International Development (USAID) began to sponsor well-drilling for the Directorate of Water Supply, the Vietnamese had been making do in the larger cities with a number of high-capacity deep wells begun in the 1930s by the French.

As a result of water supply and general sanitary conditions, the incidence of waterborne diseases was particularly high. Military planning would have to consider provisions for countering the problems of insect-transmitted diseases like malaria, dengue, and encephalitis. Cholera, hepatitis, and typhoid were common in the countryside because of a lack of trained medical personnel, adequate medical facilities, and proper sanitation. Amoebic and bacterial dysentery were as prevalent as tapeworm, hookworm, tuberculosis, and venereal diseases.

French Union troops had been affected by epidemics of schistosomiasis and leptospirosis—parasitic infections of the intestines and bladder—between 1950 and 1954, and a full 25 percent of the personnel operating in the delta region were finally debilitated. However, the incidence of these diseases could be reduced by immunization and other preventive medicine programs as well as by sanitary engineering. And the changing seasons had predictable effects not only on the varieties of diseases which would become most threatening at specified times but also on the kinds of military and engineering operations that could most effectively be conducted.

Layers of fine dust generated by heavy supply convoys traveling over unsurfaced roads during the dry months become a thick impassable quagmire as the rainy season begins. Heavy rainfall saturates and erodes all but the most carefully compacted and protected soil. Unpaved runways and storage areas become unusable. Lowland floods prevent cross-country movement by wheeled vehicles, and even tracked vehicles become road bound. Small streams become raging torrents washing out bridges, flooding over dams, carrying away roads, and clogging culverts with silt and mud. Bivouac areas are flooded, and fields of fire cleared during the dry months suddenly fill with lush foliage concealing ground movement beyond friendly perimeters. The persistent moisture causes shoe leather, tentage, and clothing to rot. Typhoons and squalls endanger shipping at exposed anchorages, snap ship-to-shore fuel lines, and make unloading operations virtually impossible. But the weather has the most significant effect on flight operations.

The dry season turns the countryside into a hot still oven. The dust generated by helicopters, airplanes, trucks, and earth-moving equipment gets into everything. Unless constant maintenance is carried on, dust wears out engines, clogs fuel and lubrication systems, wears out delicate moving parts, and settles into food and open wounds causing an entirely new series of infections and diseases. Heat debilitates combat and construction troops, and work slows down.

Troops whose mission is to operate in the mountains, along the coast, and in camps deep in the delta region must be supplied and supported. Roads must be made both safe from enemy interdiction and passable for heavily laden convoys. The original Vietnamese roads had, however, deteriorated as a result of repeated sabotage, lack of maintenance, and heavy usage. In width, alignment, and surfacing, they could not possibly support the weight and volume of increased military traffic.

How were the U.S. forces and their allies to maintain thousands of miles of roads, hundreds of bridges, and thousands of culverts without stationing engineer units in compounds throughout the length and breadth of Vietnam? How were they to support a complex modern army of half a million men without ports and depots to receive, sort, and store supplies? Where would they house this army and in what kind of structures? South Vietnam's lumber industry was nonexistent and the country's mineral resources were very low. Even the basic construction materials—sand, gravel, and rock—were not readily available.

The very nature of the war required a military presence everywhere, and that simply meant dotting the countryside with fire-support bases, maneuver-element base camps, logistic support areas, heliports, and tactical airstrips. The nature of the war imposed a distinct need for jet airfields from which ground support missions could be flown. And each base, airfield, and compound had to be joined to its neighbor in an ever-expanding network of primary and secondary roads.

CHAPTER II

Organizing the Assistance Effort

Since the inception of the United States Military Assistance Command, Vietnam, on 8 February 1962, its policies, organization, and objectives were guided by staff contingency planning for the entire Southeast Asia area. The chain of command from Military Assistance Command headquarters in Saigon to Pacific Command headquarters in Hawaii was established primarily at the insistence of Admiral Harry D. Felt, Commander in Chief, Pacific, who strongly believed that only Pacific Command with its joint Army, Navy, and Air Force staff could effectively and dispassionately deal with the entire Southeast Asia area. For this reason the staff and planning capabilities at Military Assistance Command, Vietnam (MACV), were limited. Contingency and long-term operational planning for Southeast Asia were to be conducted from the headquarters having cognizance of the entire Pacific theater. Furthermore, the disrupted political and military situation had not been accurately appraised. It was thought that the insurgency problem could be brought under control in short order and that a temporary MACV headquarters incorporating the old Military Assistance Advisory Group (MAAG) as an operating headquarters would prove adequate for handling operations until the emergency passed and the Military Assistance Advisory Group could resume its normal functioning. (*Chart 1*)

General Paul D. Harkins, as the first Commander, U.S. Military Assistance Command, Vietnam (COMUSMACV), was responsible for performing the functions of the chief of the old military advisory group and in that capacity acted as senior adviser to the Republic of Vietnam's armed forces while also commanding the Army component of the combined services' Military Assistance Command. The commanding general of the U.S. Army Support Group, Vietnam, which had been formed in 1961 to provide administrative and logistic support for Army forces in Vietnam, became the deputy Army component commander. General Harkins therefore exercised operational control of Army forces, while the commanding general of Support Group, Vietnam, was responsible for administrative and logistic support.

CHART 1—COMMAND STRUCTURE IN THE PACIFIC

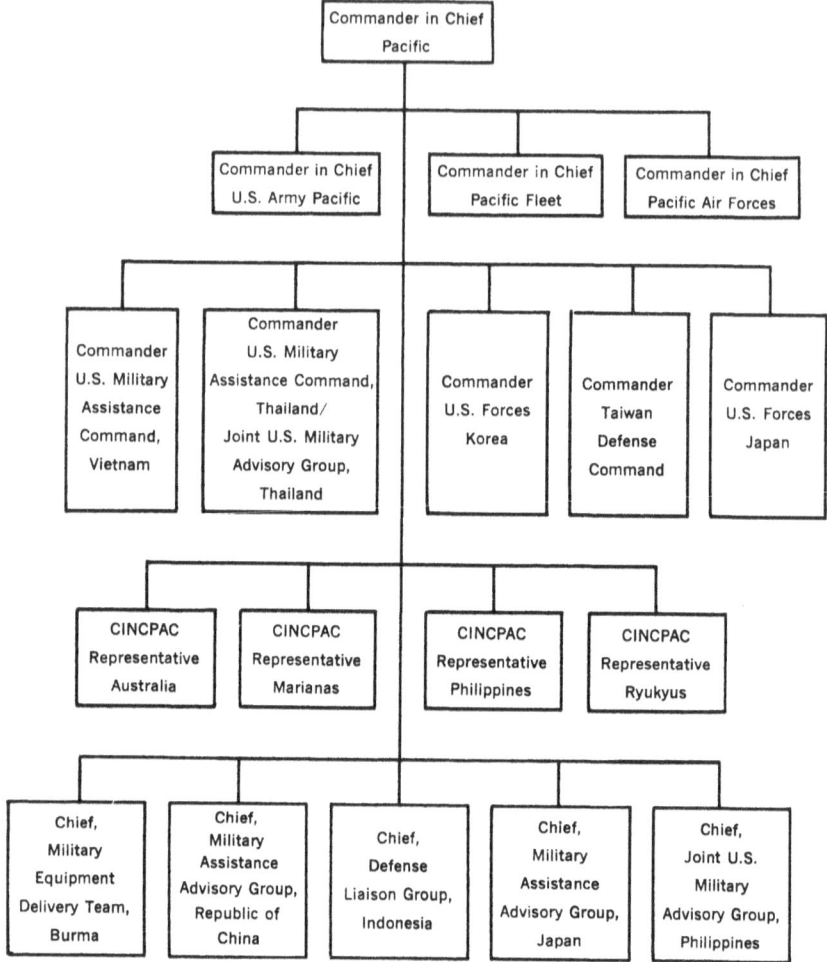

The Military Assistance Advisory Group was finally absorbed intact by the Military Assistance Command, Vietnam, in 1964. The air and naval advisory activities and their personnel were subordinated to the corresponding component commands of the Military Assistance Command. General Harkins as COMUSMACV was succeeded on 20 June 1964 by General William C. Westmoreland, who continued to direct actively only Army component activities while providing general guidance to the other participating services. Shortly after General Westmoreland assumed command, the U.S. force buildup completely outpaced the existing support system, and in April 1965 the 1st Logistical Command was deployed and subsequently assigned to the U.S. Army Support Group, Vietnam. (*Chart 2*)

When President Lyndon B. Johnson was given the mandate of Congress to commit U.S. troops in August of 1964, and the decision was made to do so on a large scale, it became apparent that a review of the command and control structures would be necessary. The major issues concerned MACV's status as a subordinate unified command under orders from Pacific Command headquarters, MACV's working relations with the Vietnamese military and arriving allies, and MACV's U.S. troop command authority.

The same argument Admiral Felt voiced in 1962 was raised

CHART 2—MACV COMMAND STRUCTURE

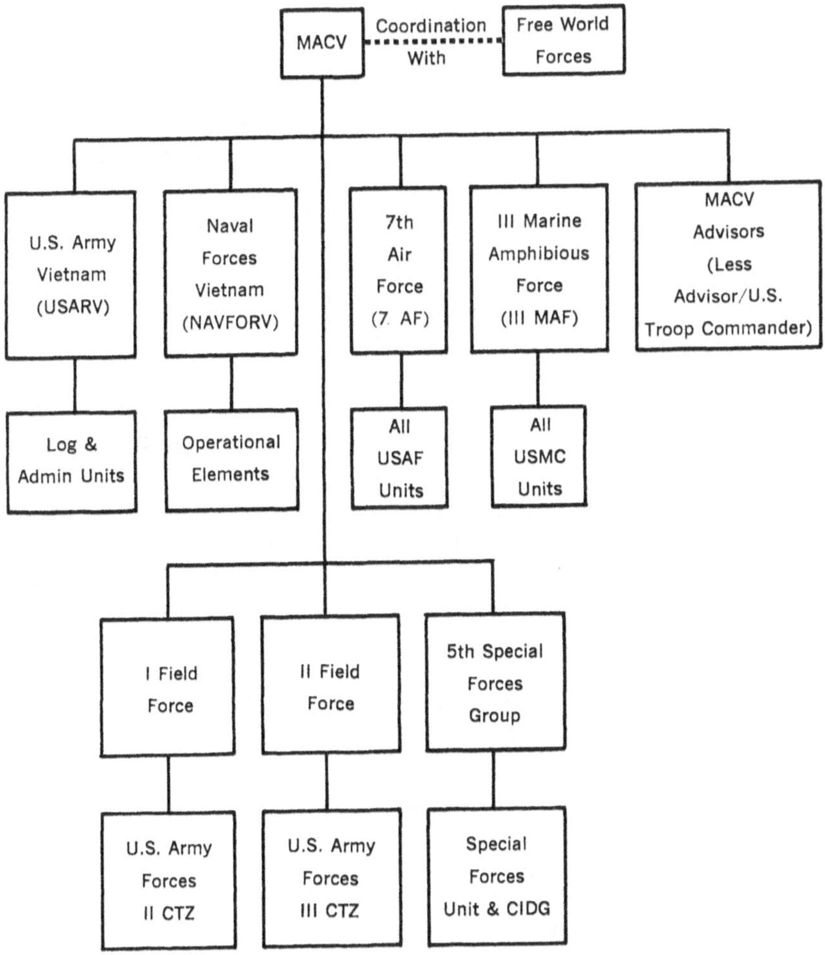

```
                                    MACV ---- Coordination ---- Free World
                                              With              Forces
    ┌───────────────┬───────────────┼───────────────┬───────────────┐
  U.S. Army       Naval           7th            III Marine       MACV
  Vietnam         Forces          Air            Amphibious       Advisors
  (USARV)         Vietnam         Force          Force            (Less
                  (NAVFORV)       (7. AF)        (III MAF)        Advisor/U.S.
                                                                  Troop Commander)
    │               │               │               │
  Log &           Operational     All             All
  Admin Units     Elements        USAF            USMC
                                  Units           Units
                                    │
                  ┌─────────────────┼─────────────────┐
                I Field           II Field          5th Special
                Force             Force             Forces Group
                  │                 │                 │
                U.S. Army         U.S. Army         Special
                Forces            Forces            Forces
                II CTZ            III CTZ           Unit & CIDG
```

again in 1965, this time by the new Commander in Chief, Pacific, Admiral U. S. Grant Sharp. The military threat in the Pacific was not limited to Vietnam and action there could not, therefore, be conducted without regard for operations and plans for Japan, Korea, the Philippines, Laos, Thailand, or any other Pacific area. Military Assistance Command would remain subordinate to Pacific Command (PACOM) headquarters, and General Westmoreland could direct his attention to Vietnam exclusively.

The second issue under consideration, MACV's relationship with the Vietnamese armed forces, was still more sensitive. A single joint command under an American commander hinted too strongly of American colonialism; therefore command would devolve into co-operation and co-ordination between U.S. and Vietnamese forces. The question of the operational control of U.S. Army forces involved both military and political considerations.

To provide administrative control of and support for the combat forces, the U.S. Army Support Command was transformed into the U.S. Army, Vietnam (USARV), on 20 July to carry out "all the functions of a field army save those an Army commander would perform at a forward command post." Military Assistance Command would carry out the tactical functions. The establishment of USARV made a headquarters available with the personnel and other resources required to control all Army activities. An Army component headquarters, exercising operational control over land combat forces, would have been in keeping with existing doctrine and, in the opinion of some observers, would have provided a more efficient means of conducting land combat operations. In the context of events in 1965, however, adoption of this approach was not so clearly indicated. In particular, it would have required General Westmoreland to interpose a new, untested, and inexperienced headquarters between himself and his newly arrived American combat troops. Of equal concern was the fact that the South Vietnamese Joint General Staff (JGS) was also the Army of Vietnam headquarters. Co-ordination of land combat operations was being conducted between MACV and the JGS; if operational control of U.S. Army forces had rested in USARV, the absence of a counterpart headquarters in the Vietnamese Army would have made co-ordination much more difficult. For these reasons, the responsibilities of USARV were limited to administrative and logistical matters.

Before mid-1965, when the first U.S. engineer units arrived, the only American construction capability in Vietnam resided in a small civilian force under contract to the Navy. For a number of years the Department of Defense had followed the practice of assigning to the construction arms of the Army, Navy, and Air Force areas of

ORGANIZING THE ASSISTANCE EFFORT

responsibility around the world where bases were planned, under way, or already built. The Army Corps of Engineers was given jurisdiction over military construction contracts in Japan, Okinawa, Taiwan, Korea, the Mediterranean, and the Near East. Air Force Civil Engineers were assigned the United Kingdom, and the Navy Bureau of Yards and Docks (which was later redesignated Naval Facilities Engineering Command) was committed to Spain, the South Pacific islands, Guantánamo Bay, Antarctica, and Southeast Asia. As Department of Defense contract construction agent, the Naval Facilities Engineering Command (NAVFAC) had an Officer in Charge of Construction (OICC) for Southeast Asia headquartered in Bangkok, Thailand, with a branch office in Saigon. In July 1965 the Navy divided the area by creating the position Officer in Charge of Construction, Republic of Vietnam.

As the military buildup gained momentum, engineer and construction forces received higher priorities for mobilization and deployment. With the arrival of contingents of Army engineers, Navy Seabees, Marine Corps engineers, Air Force Prime BEEF and Red Horse units, and civilian contractors, U.S. construction strength in Vietnam mounted rapidly. Because the buildup was so rapid, construction had to be accomplished on a crash basis, but before that could be done there were numerous logistical obstacles to overcome. Changing requirements for facilities from which to conduct or support combat operations and deployments interfered with the establishment of construction priorities, which in turn depended upon the availability of labor, equipment, materials, and sites, for which there was intense competition among the services.

During a visit to Vietnam in July 1965, the Deputy Assistant Secretary of Defense for Properties and Installations discussed the situation with the Assistant Chief of Staff for Logistics (J-4), MACV, and the commander of Military Assistance Command. He strongly urged that "there be one focal point in MACV for direction of construction matters, a central office with which the Department of Defense, CINCPAC, and other service agencies can coordinate"; and he recommended a construction czar other than the MACV J-4.

General Westmoreland had assigned staff supervision of base development to his Assistant Chief of Staff for Logistics. Up to the time of the buildup, the J-4 had been concerned primarily with the Military Assistance Program (MAP). Among other duties the J-4 also chaired the U.S. Construction Staff Committee which consisted of representatives of agencies involved in civil and military construction. Within the J-4 office was a Base Development Branch of four officers headed by a Navy commander and overly occupied for the most part with routine staff matters. About twenty-five Engineer officers were also in the Engineer Branch of the Directorate of the Army MAP Logistics—a separate staff agency and remnant of the old MAAG. Headed by Colonel Kenneth W. Kennedy, Corps of Engineers, this branch had the mission of advising the Vietnamese Armed Forces Chief of Engineers. On 7 April 1965, J-4 merged the Engineer Branch, Directorate of Army MAP Logistics, with its small Base Development Branch to form the Engineer Division, J-4, under Colonel Kennedy; but, as the scope of engineer activities (especially base development) expanded, the post of the Engineer was upgraded to Deputy J-4 for Engineering in November 1965.

During this same month Secretary of Defense Robert S. McNamara visited General Westmoreland's headquarters in Saigon, where he was advised that the then-envisaged construction program would cost about $1 billion within a two-year period. Upon his return to Washington, Secretary McNamara directed the establishment of a construction base for Vietnam. On 11 February 1966 the position of Director of Construction (MACDC) was established. As a special staff officer, he would report directly to General Westmoreland independently of J-4 channels. Brigadier General Carroll H. Dunn, who had been selected for promotion to major general, was the first director and served in this post until 1966 when he was succeeded by his deputy, Brigadier General Daniel A. Raymond. General Dunn's initial staff consisted of 135 people, half Army, one-quarter Navy, and one-quarter Air Force. The mission assigned to General Dunn was to "direct, manage, and supervise the combined and coordinated construction program to meet MACV requirements and coordinate all Department of Defense construction efforts and resources assigned to MACV or in the Republic of Vietnam."

The ultimate mission of the MACV Director of Construction was to provide military engineering advice and assistance to the Commander, U.S. Military Assistance Command, Vietnam. In executing this mission the Construction Directorate supervised the construction program; co-ordinated all Department of Defense construction efforts and resources assigned to Military Assistance Command or other agencies in Vietnam; established joint service policy; and monitored all military construction programs. The Construction Directorate also supervised the execution of interservice facility management matters and obtained and allocated real estate for use by U.S. and Free World Military Assistance Forces. The Construction Directorate was later given the responsibility for advising and assisting the Ministry of Public Works, Communications, and Transportation relative to the government of Vietnam's highway and road system. The directorate also assisted the component services, the Agency for International Development, and the Vietnamese National Railway System in the development of waterways and railways.

The establishment of the Director of Construction clarified several matters: the Commander, Military Assistance Command, would exercise direct control of the construction effort in Vietnam, including direction of the Navy's Officer in Charge of Construction in areas of project assignments, priorities of effort, and standards of construction. He would control the use and allocation of all construction resources in Vietnam. What up to now had been several programs of separate agencies responsible to different bosses both in and out of Vietnam became a unified program under centralized control and direction.

Throughout 1965 there had been an increased commitment of U.S. military personnel. On 8 March 1965, 3,500 marines landed in the I Corps area to take up defensive positions around the U.S. air base at Da Nang. On 5 May 1965, U.S. Air Force C–130 aircraft began landing at Bien Hoa Air Base, north of Saigon, with the main body of the 173d Airborne Brigade, previously stationed on Okinawa. On 16 June 1965, the Secretary of Defense announced the deployment of an additional 21,000 U.S. troops to South Vietnam, which brought the total commitment to 75,000.

On 12 July, the 2d Brigade, 1st Infantry Division, landed at Vung Tau and immediately moved inland to Bien Hoa. To the north, the 2d Brigade's remaining battalion came ashore at Cam Ranh Bay and relieved the 1st Logistical Command forces of the bulk of the peninsula security mission. A little over two weeks later, the 1st Brigade, 101st Airborne Division, landed at Cam Ranh Bay and relieved a battalion of the 2d Brigade, 1st Division, of its security mission. These two brigades were the first U.S. Army combat forces to be deployed from the United States to South Vietnam.

On 28 July 1965, in a television address to the nation the President announced: "I have today ordered to Vietnam . . . forces which will raise our fighting strength from 75,000 to 125,000 men almost immediately. Additional forces will be needed later and they will be sent as requested." In the next five months, the strength of U.S. forces rose not to 125,000 but to nearly 200,000. By Christmas 1965, the 1st Cavalry Division (Airmobile) and the 1st Infantry Division (–) had arrived in South Vietnam, where they were joined by the Korean 1st (Capital-Tiger) Infantry Division. To control the U.S. combat forces in II Corps, Task Force Alpha, a corps head-

ELEMENTS OF 1ST CAVALRY DIVISION (AIRMOBILE) *arrive at Qui Nhon September 1965.*

quarters, was deployed in August from Fort Hood, Texas, to Nha Trang.

The troop buildup continued into the new year. On 29 December 1965 the 3d Brigade, 25th Infantry Division, began a two-week movement from Schofield Barracks, Hawaii, to Pleiku. By 8 January 1966 a second corps headquarters, designated II Field Force, was deployed to manage U.S. combat forces in the III and IV Corps areas.

The first Army engineer unit to arrive in Vietnam was the 173d Engineer Company, which landed at Bien Hoa on 5 May 1965 as part of the 173d Airborne Brigade. This company, like other brigade and divisional engineer units, worked to establish base camps and provide combat support to the larger organization of which it was a part.

On 9 June 1965 Headquarters, 35th Engineer Group, together with the 864th Engineer Battalion and D Company, 84th Engineers, had debarked on the Cam Ranh Peninsula. These were the first major units to arrive at Cam Ranh Bay. On 16 July the 159th Engineer Group (Construction) at Fort Bragg, North Carolina,

ORGANIZING THE ASSISTANCE EFFORT

received orders to activate Headquarters, 18th Engineer Brigade, from its resources. On 30 July the newly formed brigade received movement orders, and one month later it departed for South Vietnam and assignment to U.S. Army, Vietnam. This brigade was commanded by Brigadier General Robert R. Ploger. The brigade's advance party arrived in Vietnam on 3 September and immediately scrambled to find space in the Saigon area for its headquarters and to establish a communications net with its subordinate units. On 16 September the headquarters (less the main body, which did not arrive until 21 September) became operational and assumed command of all nondivisional Army engineer units from the 1st Logistical Command. In northern II Corps, meanwhile, the engineer situation was significantly changed by the arrival at Qui Nhon of Headquarters, 937th Engineer Group (Combat), and the 70th Engineer Battalion (Combat) on 23 August. These units came to Southeast Asia as time-tested organizations, since both had been in operation before deploying. By 1 October 1965 the engineer force was composed of two group headquarters, six battalions, and nine separate companies. One week later USARV assigned the following missions to the brigade:

> a. Provide operational planning and supervision of USARV construction and related tasks in the Republic of Vietnam and for other missions as may be directed by this headquarters.
>
> b. Exercise command and operational control of engineer units assigned to United States Army, Vietnam.
>
> c. Provide for physical security of personnel, equipment, facilities, and construction of all units assigned or attached to your command.

On 1 January 1966 the 20th and 39th Engineer Battalions, along with the 572d Light Equipment Company, landed at Cam Ranh Bay. From 2 January until mid-May, only two companies were added to the strength of the 18th Brigade. The 20th and 39th Battalions were the last products of the initial herculean push by the United States Continental Army Command to deploy a maximum number of engineer units to Southeast Asia. It would be summer before the steady flow of engineers across the Pacific would resume.

The command situation for base development was by now formally established. The Director of Construction at the MACV joint staff headquarters exercised control and guidance for all service construction. Air Force, Navy, and Army construction efforts would be co-ordinated through this office. To ensure effective operation, the Construction Directorate was organized along functional lines. The directorate originally consisted of five main divisions: Plans and Operations, Engineering and Base Development, Construction Management, Real Estate, and Program Management. On 1 January 1968 a major revision of the organization occurred with the creation of the Lines of Communications (LOC) Division. *(Chart 3)* The LOC Division assumed the responsibility for managing a 4,100-kilometer road restoration program and for advising the Vietnamese Director General of Highways. Before this reorganization, LOC responsibility had been delegated to the Construction Management

CHART 3—ORGANIZATION OF MACDC, 1968

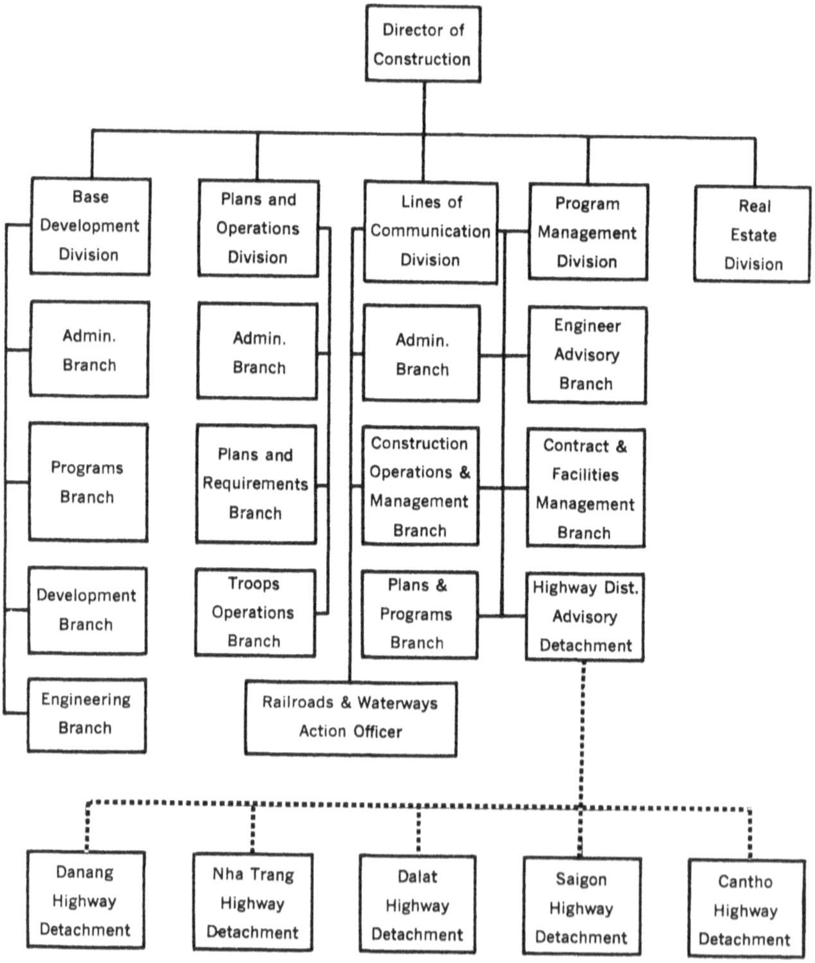

```
                        Director of
                        Construction
                             |
   ┌─────────────┬─────────────┬─────────────┬─────────────┐
   │             │             │             │             │
Base         Plans and      Lines of     Program        Real
Development  Operations     Communication Management    Estate
Division     Division       Division     Division       Division
   │             │             │             │
Admin.       Admin.         Admin.       Engineer
Branch       Branch         Branch       Advisory
                                         Branch
   │             │             │             │
Programs     Plans and      Construction Contract &
Branch       Requirements   Operations & Facilities
             Branch         Management   Management
                            Branch       Branch
   │             │             │             │
Development  Troops         Plans &      Highway Dist.
Branch       Operations     Programs     Advisory
             Branch         Branch       Detachment
   │             │
Engineering  Railroads & Waterways
Branch       Action Officer
                             │
   ┌──────────┬──────────┬──────────┬──────────┐
Danang     Nha Trang  Dalat      Saigon     Cantho
Highway    Highway    Highway    Highway    Highway
Detachment Detachment Detachment Detachment Detachment
```

ORGANIZING THE ASSISTANCE EFFORT

Division, which was dissolved. Its functions were assumed by the Base Development Division.

The Base Development Division served as the focal point for base development planning, for monitoring the component service base construction projects, and for interservice facility management matters. Engineer staff activities pertaining to military operation, determination of engineer requirements and plans for employment of engineer forces, and technical supervision of engineer activities were the responsibility of the Plans and Operation Division.

The Lines of Communications Division, once established, directed, supervised, and managed the development and restoration of designated roads to support military operations, pacification programs, and national economic growth. The division co-ordinated the planning and execution of LOC programs for the component services, the Agency for International Development, and the Vietnamese government. Assistance and advisory support were also provided to the Ministry of Public Works, Communications, and Transportation; to the Directorate General of Highways; and to the five regional engineers and the province engineers. The Lines of Communications Division also assisted all interested agencies in the development of waterways and railways. The Program Management Branch, meanwhile, was responsible for funding matters including fund status, piaster impact, and statistical analysis of the Vietnamese military construction program, while the Real Estate Division served as the MACV agent in obtaining and allocating real estate for U.S. use.

The commander of Army units in Vietnam remained the Commanding General, U.S. Army, Vietnam. As senior Army component commander, he was responsible for base development at ports, beaches, depots, and major installations in II, III, and IV Corps Tactical Zones, except for those bases specifically assigned to other services through the office of the MACV Director of Construction. Since the Commanding General, U.S. Army, Vietnam, was also the Commander, Military Assistance Command, Vietnam, this apparent division of command may be seen as a simple differentiation of staff functions made necessary by the diversity of responsibilities inherent in the planning staff, which was MACV, and the execution staff, which was USARV.

Initially the Army engineer construction effort was the responsibility of the Engineer Section of the 1st Logistical Command. In September 1965 the headquarters of the 18th Engineer Brigade arrived and assumed responsibility of engineer staff planning from the 1st Logistical Command; the Commanding General, 18th Engineer Brigade, acted as both the Engineer Troop Commander and the Army Engineer until December 1966 when the U.S. Army Engineer Command was formed. The 18th Engineer Brigade was then delegated the responsibility for engineer support in I and II Corps Tactical Zones. The Engineer Command took over responsibility for over-all supervision of the Army construction program and direct supervision of two engineer groups operating in II and IV Corps Tactical Zones. When the 20th Engineer Brigade arrived in Vietnam and was delegated the responsibility of engineer support in III and IV Corps Tactical Zones, the Engineer Command functioned as the over-all planning staff for Army construction subordinate to the Engineer, USARV. In March 1968 the Engineer Command was reorganized with the U.S. Army Engineer Construction Agency, Vietnam (USAECAV), and was charged with responsibility for managing and administering real estate, property maintenance, and execution of the Military Construction, Army (MCA), construction programs. At the same time the Office of the Engineer, USARV, served as the component staff engineer.

The Engineer's staff at USARV headquarters consisted of five main divisions: Construction, Facilities Engineering, Mapping and Intelligence, Military Operations, and Supply and Maintenance. (*Chart 4*) Although the organizational structure of the Construction Agency provided for operational independence, policies and proce-

CHART 4—USARV ENGINEER ORGANIZATION

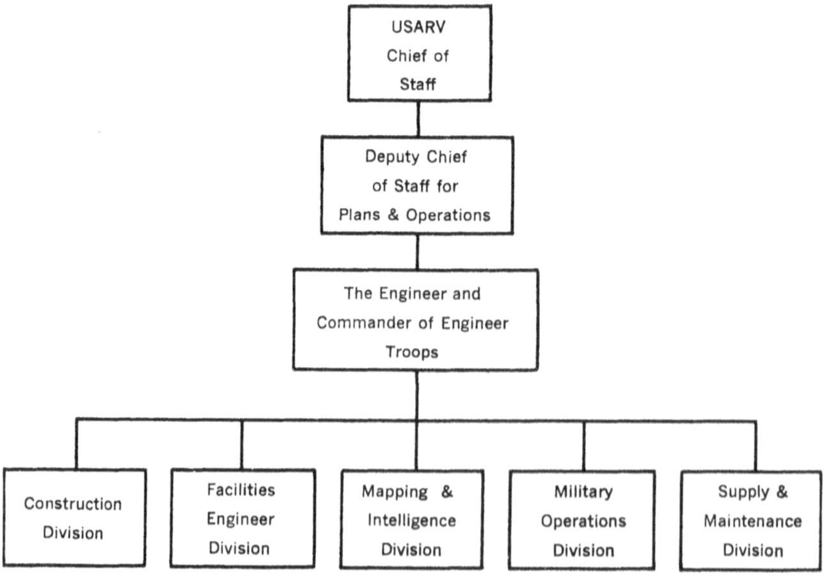

```
            USARV
           Chief of
            Staff
              |
        Deputy Chief
        of Staff for
      Plans & Operations
              |
       The Engineer and
     Commander of Engineer
             Troops
              |
   ┌──────┬──────┬──────┬──────┬──────┐
Construction Facilities Mapping &  Military  Supply &
  Division  Engineer  Intelligence Operations Maintenance
            Division   Division    Division   Division
```

dures were prescribed by U.S. Army in Vietnam. The Construction Agency at Army headquarters was composed of three main divisions: Engineering, Real Estate, and Real Property Management. The USAECAV organization also utilized the area concept and had district offices in four major geographical locations.

Like the Construction Agency, the engineer brigades were subordinate to the U.S. Army in Vietnam and their organization and mission evolved in an area concept. The brigades each operated in two tactical zones. Since the brigades divided their areas into group and battalion areas of operations, the battalions were responsible for all engineer support within assigned areas of operation.

Naval construction planning at the beginning of the buildup was delegated to the III Marine Amphibious Force. In October 1965, III Marine Amphibious Force was provided a small support activity which was an extension of Services Forces, Pacific, and the Director of the Pacific Division of Bureau of Yards and Docks. This activity assumed the responsibility for facility planning until April 1966 when the Commander, Naval Forces, Vietnam (COMNAVFORV), assumed the duties of co-ordinator and planner for base, port, beach, depot, air base, road, and installation construction for all Navy, Marine, and allied forces operating in I Corps and for other distinct naval operations in II, III, and IV Corps areas.

The Commander, Naval Forces, Vietnam, as the Navy component commander, was placed under operational control of the Commander, Military Assistance Command, Vietnam, but remained under the operational command of the Commander in Chief, Pacific Fleet, the operating naval force of the Commander in Chief, Pacific.

The Department of Defense contract construction agent in Vietnam, the Navy's Officer in Charge of Construction, had been providing construction resources. This office and its organization had been modified frequently since 1962 when the Navy negotiated a $16.5 million cost-plus-a-fixed-fee contract with a joint contractor, Raymond International and Morrison-Knudsen (RMK), for construction of airfields and port facilities in Vietnam to support the country's armed forces. The buildup of American forces increased the scope of contract construction. In August 1965 RMK brought two additional contractors—Brown & Root and J. A. Jones—into the partnership (henceforth referred to as RMK–BRJ) to bolster personnel strength and management capability. Lyman D. Wilbur, vice president of Morrison-Knudsen, was in charge of work from May 1965 until February 1966, when he was succeeded by Bert Perkins, also a vice president of the same corporation.

The Navy's OICC in supervising the RMK–BRJ contract assigned a Naval Civil Engineering Corps officer as resident officer in charge at each major construction site. The OICC since 1965 had been a Navy flag officer of the Civil Engineer Corps.

Unlike the other services, the Air Force was able to avoid many construction planning difficulties. The 7th Air Force Civil Engineer Directorate possessed the planning force required for its construction program in Vietnam before the 1965 buildup, and the 7th Air Force was responsible only for base development at air bases and at other installations where the Air Force was designated as having a primary mission.

The Army's responsibility for facilities engineering support before 1965 was limited to six MACV advisory sites located outside Saigon. The Navy's Headquarters Support Activity, Saigon, took care of all military property within the city. But because of a lack of trained military personnel and experience in contracting for facilities engineering in Korea, the Army decided to contract for this support at the MACV advisory sites. Seven firms submitted bids, and negotiations were undertaken with four of them. On 1 May 1963, Pacific Architects and Engineers (PA&E) received a cost-plus-a-fixed-fee contract.

This contract, except for a change in the type of fee, was the kind awarded as the buildup continued. The contractor was to provide all facilities engineering support for the Army in Vietnam and was to establish an organization essentially the same as provided in Army regulations for standard facilities engineering units. The contractor was to furnish the labor, organization, and management; the government was to supply equipment, repair parts, tools, and material as well as quarters and messing facilities. The flexibility of this contract proved invaluable in the years ahead.

While considerable attention is given in this text to the deployment of Army engineer units, it should be recognized that these units actually constituted less than half of the total American construction force in Vietnam. By mid-1968, thirty-five engineer battalions, forty-two separate companies, and numerous teams and detachments had been deployed. At its peak, Army engineer strength in Vietnam approximated 40,000 officers and men, including members of combat engineer units of the seven Army divisions and six separate brigades and regiments.

The following summary sets forth what might be termed the construction force in Vietnam. Essentially it lists the principal agencies involved in construction in South Vietnam, and therefore the agencies whose construction activities were co-ordinated, integrated, and directed to varying degrees by the MACV Director of Construction.

ORGANIZING THE ASSISTANCE EFFORT

U.S. Army

1. Army Engineer Command (Provisional). Consisted of 2 brigades, 6 groups, 21 battalions, and various small specialized engineer units.
2. Pacific Architects and Engineers. Under contract for repairs and utilities support of the Army (21,418 personnel).
3. DeLong Corporation. Fabricated and installed patented mobile piers.
4. Vinnell Corporation. Constructed, operated, and maintained electrical systems including T-2 tankers used as power sources.

U.S. Air Force

1. Walter Kidde Constructors. Employed on a turnkey basis to design and construct Tuy Hoa Air Base.
2. Red Horse Squadrons. Five light construction squadrons structured for augmentation by local labor.
3. Base Emergency Engineering Forces (BEEF) Teams. Small detachments which contained a high level of skills and capability of constructing small quantities of critical facilities.
4. Base Civil Engineering Forces. Equipped to handle repairs and utilities at established bases.

U.S. Naval Forces

1. One construction brigade, composed of the 30th Naval Construction Regiment with nine Seabee battalions.
2. Three engineer construction battalions of the Fleet Marine Force, USMC.
3. Naval Support Activity, Public Works Forces.
4. Philco. Under contract to provide a labor force.
5. Naval Facilities Engineering Command
    a. Office in Charge of Construction (OICC), RVN. OICC supervised and administered the contract for:
    b. RMK-BRJ. This joint venture of four American contractors accomplished the largest portion of construction projects.

Other U.S. agencies in the organization for construction were those of the embassy's Office of Civil Operations and the MACV Revolutionary Development Support Directorate.

Until early 1967, there was a tendency to view the reconstruction phase of pacification as a Vietnamese effort, supported by U.S. civil agencies, while the U.S. military command concentrated on building Vietnamese combat capabilities. Integration and co-ordination were lacking among the several U.S. civil agencies involved. The U.S.

Agency for International Development (USAID), the Joint United States Public Affairs Office (JUSPAO), and the Office of the Special Assistant to the Ambassador (OSA), and the military agencies sometimes worked at cross-purposes. To correct this defect the Civil Operations and Rural Development Support (CORDS) structure was formed under MACV to provide single manager control of U.S. military and civilian efforts in support of Vietnamese pacification programs. CORDS did not include all of the advisory efforts of OSA and JUSPAO. These organizations continued to supply some construction material to the Vietnamese for self-help, while military units often performed the actual reconstruction.

CHAPTER III

Real Estate and Land Acquisition

The United States acquired "rent-free" real estate in Vietnam through the 1950 Agreement for Mutual Defense Assistance in Indochina, or the Pentalateral Agreement, for Free World Military Assistance Forces. Signatories to the agreement were the United States, the Republic of Vietnam, France, Laos, and Cambodia. Although Article IV of the agreement spelled out what real estate the United States would be provided, as late as 1969 the U.S. Embassy's position was not to push for full Vietnamese compliance, based on the belief that the agreement as signed did not provide for, or envision, operations occurring after 1965.

As a result of high-level diplomatic discussions in 1965, the government of Vietnam did agree to assume responsibility for all land acquisition, funding for payments, and relocations without directly charging the United States. The cost would be covered by continued American support of the deficit in the Vietnamese budget. The Interior Ministerial Real Estate Committee (IMREC) was established to acquire and provide American and other Free World military forces with unimproved rent-free real estate. Tabulations of owners, amounts of real estate affected by land acquisition, determination of the amounts of indemnification, and actual payments were made by the Vietnamese government without overt American participation.

General Westmoreland's staff became the agency for dealing with the Vietnamese government in the acquisition of real estate for allied armed forces in Vietnam. The Director of Construction was after 15 February 1966 responsible to the commander of Military Assistance Command for the performance of these functions. The Navy and Air Force component commanders at Military Assistance Command were directed by General Westmoreland to co-ordinate real-estate functions and activities of all allied forces within their areas of responsibility.

An Engineer Division of the MACV J–4 was organized during late April 1965, and a Real Estate Branch within this division came into being on 2 May 1965. The 64th Engineer Detachment (Terrain) was placed under operational control of COMUSMACV, and its assets consisting of five officers and five enlisted men were used to establish a Real Estate Branch within the Engineer Division. On 15 February 1966, when the Construction Directorate was established, this same real-estate organization was structured into the directorate and continued discharging the responsibility for co-ordinating all real-estate activities within Vietnam.

The Director of Construction, MACV, continued to receive all requests for real estate, except lease requests, to support U.S. and other Free World military forces and transmitted them to the Vietnamese Joint General Staff, which returned them, approved or disapproved, to the requesting component commanders through the MACV staff. The Director of Construction allocated available real estate to elements of allied military forces. He also maintained a central inventory of all leased and rent-free real estate and was responsible for returning Vietnamese-owned property to the government when it was no longer required.

The various component commanders were given the responsibility of co-ordinating real-estate transactions for base development in their operational areas. The Commander, 7th Air Force, was responsible for all air bases where the Air Force had the primary mission. The Commander, Naval Forces, Vietnam, managed the I Corps area exclusive of the bases assigned to the Air Force, and the Commanding General, U.S. Army, Vietnam, managed II, III, and IV Corps except for Air Force bases.

MACV followed, insofar as possible, the Pacific Army headquarters' regulations for real-estate policy and procedures, which were published in December of 1965. General Westmoreland, as Commanding General, U.S. Army, Vietnam, made the commanding officer of the 1st Logistical Command responsible for the acquisition, recording, reporting, and disposal of real estate for those units assigned or attached to U.S. Army, Vietnam. The USARV Engineer exercised staff supervision for procedures governing real-estate leasing as carried out by 1st Logistical Command. The 1st Logistical Command's responsibility for real estate was continued until April 1968 when Major General William T. Bradley, Commanding General, U.S. Army Engineer Construction Agency, Vietnam (USAECAV), was delegated the responsibility.

A Central Real Estate Office (CREO) was established in Saigon to administer leases and act as the repository for master leases. Area real estate offices (AREO's) were established in U.S. Army Support Command logistics areas. Area offices were located in Qui Nhon, Nha Trang, Vung Tau, and Can Tho. Two more offices were set up in Saigon, and one of these was responsible solely for the Headquarters Area Command (the greater Saigon area). Customer contact, whether for rent-free or leased property, was made with the AREO. The area real estate office processed land-use requests and negotiated leases only when authorized by the Central Real Estate Office.

Pacific Army headquarters delegated acquisition approval authority to the Commanding General, USARV, for leasing real estate when the contract was renewable annually and the total annual rental did not exceed $300,000. This authority was redelegated to the 1st Logistical Command and later to the Commanding General, U.S. Army Construction Agency, Vietnam, when he assumed the real-estate mission. The chief of the Real Estate Division at CREO and later at USAECAV headquarters at Long Binh, became a contracting officer for real-estate matters with a $100,000 contract authority, since about 90 percent of the leases cost less than $100,000 annually.

Augmented by an office staff of contract employees of the Pacific Architects and Engineers, Inc. (PA&E), the Real Estate Division also received, processed, and made utility payments which averaged about $2 million annually. The division was also responsible for preparation and submission of the reports based on real property and feeder information sent in from contract and military post engineer organizations throughout Vietnam. These reports were the basis of the real-estate inventories maintained at higher headquarters.

For a unit to acquire property a unique request system was operated. The unit would initiate a Land-Use Request containing a description of the property and justification for its acquisition. With the request a note of concurrence or rejection was forwarded by the local government official responsible for that area. These officials included province chiefs, district chiefs, mayors of autonomous cities, and military region, base, or unit commanders. The request was then forward to the chairman of the Interior Ministerial Real Estate Committee by Military Assistance Command. Written approval, or a Land-Use Concurrence, from the Vietnamese provided MACV rent-free use of the property as long as the requirement existed.

Occupation of real estate without Vietnamese approval created several problems. Primarily the Vietnamese government could not compensate land owners for appropriated land unless requests for land were sent through proper channels. Unless a request went through MACV to the Interior Ministerial Real Estate Committee, no funds were transferred to the property owners.

In many instances, real estate was used and developed immediately upon submission of the land-use request based on the concurrence of a local Vietnamese official. Yet some of these requests were never acted on by the government, which usually did not have sufficient funds for indemnification. At other times action was deferred because of political influence. Regardless of action, nearly all the land requests stated that upon termination of use and occupancy of the real estate, Military Assistance Command retained the option of removing or abandoning in place any installation on it. Vietnamese government approval further stipulated that when MACV no longer had need of the real estate it would be returned to the Vietnamese armed forces along with all improvements. This difference was never negotiated, and real estate was acquired for air bases, base camps, logistics complexes, and industrial sites for asphalt plants, crushers, concrete plants, and administrative space; easements were also acquired for utilities, roads, and communications cables. Each land-use concurrence varied in size from single office locations to bases like Chu Lai, which was 26 million square meters of cleared land.

Initially it had been necessary to obtain concurrences for road improvement projects and new road construction, but with the advent of the MACV Lines of Communications (LOC) program, the Vietnamese government assumed the responsibility of providing real estate for jointly used roads. This took the component commanders out of the real estate acquisition business at least for this program.

In support of tactical operations, land-clearing projects required no real-estate action, nor was it necessary to transact for real estate which was occupied during combat operations. Claims arising from the use, occupancy, or damages during and after military operations were handled by the U.S. Army, Vietnam, Foreign Claims Division.

Although it had been stated that the Vietnamese government would furnish rent-free the real estate required for support of allied forces, this policy was generally applied only for requirements outside urban areas. In urban areas, particularly for property that was privately owned and already improved, extensive leasing was necessary. At its peak, the U.S. leasing program had an annual cost of over $20 million.

Early MACV and USARV real-estate regulations touched the leasing aspects of the program only lightly. When it became apparent that significant real-estate requirements had to be satisfied by leasing, regulations were published to cover the program. For acquisition of rent-free properties, the Vietnamese government dealt with Vietnamese owners; for acquisition of leased properties, U.S. military personnel negotiated with Vietnamese owners.

The necessity of responding to immediate needs for facilities, that is, warehousing or hotels for billets, created a sellers market. Unfortunately, there was an acute shortage of military personnel trained in the negotiation of leases. Nevertheless, what the military negotiators lacked in sophistication, they made up for in enthusiasm and responsiveness.

Because the situation was urgent, lengthy negotiations could not be conducted, and a highly undesirable condition was aggravated by other critical factors. In many areas, the number of facilities available or usable was extremely limited. Vietnamese standards of living, hence construction standards, were very different from U.S. standards, and American textbooks, manuals, and Army regulations took little cognizance of these differences. Physical security was always in question, and how to deal with the Vietnamese landlords and many other enterprising entrepreneurs not disinclined to take advantage of their tenants was always a problem.

This set of circumstances resulted in many hundreds of inadequately researched, poorly written, expensive, and badly documented leases. Yet, the results must be examined in context and should not be seriously criticized. It was remarkable that in spite of the many frustrating problems faced, real-estate personnel met needs in a timely manner.

The management of real property, once acquired, necessarily varied depending on the area, the situation, the commander, and the type of properties involved. In addition to rent-free properties, there were at one time over 900 leased properties recorded. They varied in size from large hotels to small individual villas and other facilities like cold storage spaces, warehouses, shops, and piers.

The Real Estate Division was extremely limited in its ability to manage real estate. Local commanders had to assume the burden of the task, and so real management became the direct responsibility of the installation co-ordinator, who was usually the senior officer in an area or at an installation. Installation co-ordinator positions were designated by the Commanding General, USARV, as responsible for seeing to the proper use and maintenance of all real estate at an installation. The Real Estate Division did administratively manage all leases and, within its resources, checked all properties, but management of real-estate holdings was made unusually difficult for a number of reasons. There was a great dispersion of property even within the areas serviced by any one area real-estate office. There was difficulty in traveling to properties. There was a lack of properly trained real-estate personnel. And operations were taking place in an inflationary economy. The inadequate local post engineer system was not able to maintain real property records. Requirements to follow Army regulations mainly directed at continental

U.S. (CONUS) real-estate activities and not modified for combat zone operations were in effect. Poor documentation and inventories resulted from an urgency in acquiring real estate during the buildup. Changes in personnel which occurred because of the twelve-month tour did not contribute to continuity of information. There was a very serious lack of property accountability. As time went on, the Real Estate Division began a review to try to put everything in order. Under the Engineer Construction Agency, the pieces were finally fairly well put together.

The agency instituted many improvement programs. A special title search program was started to document all properties. Many leases had been signed with persons who had not been required to prove ownership. Some properties were found to be government-owned, hence their leases were terminated and the properties used on a rent-free basis. Other contracts were terminated with lessors who could not produce a title.

Many leases had annual advance payment clauses, and this meant that when they were terminated the Army lost money. There was no procedure by which the United States could bring suit against the Vietnamese lessor for return of advance payments. An intense program was begun, however, to recoup advance payments, and it was amazingly successful considering the Real Estate Division had to rely on persuasion rather than law. Some agreements were signed in which the Army agreed to accept repayment from lessors on an installment plan. One such agreement extended over seven years.

Action was taken to renegotiate lease holdings on property for which there was a continued requirement and to reduce advance annual payments to quarterly payments. To keep the status of the changing real-estate picture up to date, to be able to terminate leases, to make payments on a more timely basis, and to increase identification and documentation of real-estate holdings, a program was developed making maximum use of automated data processing. Monthly print-outs were a valuable tool at all levels.

Dual leases, or the issuing of two leases for the same piece of real estate, one for the structure and one for the furnishings, were also a problem. The Vietnamese lessor wanted to use dual leases quite simply as a tax dodge. Although in most cases the combined price of the two leases was a fair market price for the property, it required twice as much administrative effort, the legality was highly suspect, and we indirectly contributed to the lessor's tax evasion. In cases where furnished facilities continued to be required, the contract was renegotiated in a single lease. In facilities where furnishings were no longer needed, leases were terminated at savings to the American taxpayer.

Property accountability was finally improved by transferring responsibility for maintaining the real property record cards from the Real Estate Division to the installation post engineer office. It was then the installation co-ordinator's responsibility to receipt property to the user. A Real Estate Division Utilization Branch was established to inspect leased properties and ensure their proper use. A standard lease form was developed and put into use. A series of standard operating procedures were published and distributed to explain fully real-estate operations in Vietnam. Last, a training program for military personnel was initiated in conjunction with the Office of the Chief of Engineers. Officers selected for real-estate assignments in Vietnam went to the Chief of Engineers' office in Washington, D.C., en route to Vietnam for three days of briefing and study. In Vietnam they were usually assigned to one of the branches in Real Estate Division headquarters for one or two months before going to an area office to become the point of customer contact.

In addition to the unusual conditions and unique real-estate aspects involved, there were other special problems. Acquisitions of real estate on which there were gravesites caused serious complications. Although relocation of the graves was a Vietnamese government responsibility, finding descendants was often difficult and relocation slow. Some construction was delayed for extended periods because of gravesites in the construction area. All real-estate actions were guided and influenced by the political and private considerations of the parties involved as well as by military requirements.

Our last problem was one of co-ordination. Although the U.S. Embassy rental ceilings established in 1965 were supposedly applicable to all U.S. personnel and agencies in Vietnam, it appeared that only the U.S. military seriously endeavored to comply. Many agencies had a great deal of autonomy and seemed to pay little attention to embassy policy, especially in areas where properties were scarce. Later, between 1968 and 1969, the embassy became more active in controlling interagency competition and developed a working real-estate committee on which most agencies were represented.

There were a number of lessons learned as a result of our real-estate venture in Vietnam. Certainly the absence of a working, enforceable country-to-country agreement for supplying all real estate on a rent-free basis delayed base development in some instances and resulted in a cumbersome leasing program. Furthermore, our surprisingly rapid buildup combined with a lack of appreciation on some commanders' parts for their responsibilities made it very difficult to predict new or manage old locations accurately. This condition was further aggravated by the paucity of experienced real-estate personnel, the use of CONUS-oriented regulations, and the understandable reluctance of units to give up leased civilian facilities.

To prevent similar problems in future operations, a single headquarters should be responsible for all real transactions from the start. Specially trained teams must be available to augment planning, and country-to-country agreements must be in effect sometime before the initiation of troop movements.

CHAPTER IV

Planning and the Construction Concept

The authority for setting construction priorities within the Republic of Vietnam was delegated by Admiral Sharp to General Westmoreland. As a result, the MACV logistical support plan of 1965 specified the following construction priorities: first, improve airfields and related facilities at specified locations; second, improve main supply routes; third, improve railroads as required; fourth, rehabilitate and expand port facilities at specified locations; and fifth, improve logistic base and support facilities to include petroleum, oil, and lubricants (POL) storage and dispensing facilities. In the event that any of these tasks could not be accomplished because of enemy action or for any other reason, the succeeding task would assume the higher priority.

Admiral Sharp's plan specified that facilities would be austere and that only essential operations and support facilities needed immediately would be included in the construction program. Supporting plans included real estate and facility requirements. However, this initial development plan was overtaken by the sudden and continuing increase of combat forces arriving. Once troops were ashore and deployed, bases had to be developed to sustain them. Fundamental to combat support was reliance on deep-draft vessels for shipment of bulk tonnage from the United States. Aircraft alone could never support the forces being assembled.

Before 1965 essentially all cargo entering Vietnam in deep-draft vessels came through the port of Saigon, the only port with deep-draft berths, for distribution to the rest of the country by either rail or coastal steamer. With the buildup, three factors negated this approach to logistics support for arriving U.S. forces. The tonnage required far exceeded the capacity of the port at Saigon. The railway as a system was not operational, and transshipment via coastal vessels from a single discharge point was neither economical nor feasible. The only answer to the logistics problem was to build more deep-draft ports. Fortunately, there were sufficient suitable locations where these ports could be developed.

Initially, three ports were considered to be sufficient for receiving the logistics that were originally scheduled—Da Nang in the north,

Cam Ranh Bay on the central coast, and Saigon in the south. Da Nang and Cam Ranh Bay were fine natural harbors that could be developed into ports capable of docking deep-draft oceangoing vessels with a reasonable amount of effort and cost. Saigon presented fewer possibilities, since it was a restricted river port with limited sites for additional berth development. From each of these ports then, several satellite shallow-draft coastal ports could be supported: Hue and Chu Lai from Da Nang; Qui Nhon, Nha Trang, and Phan Rang from Cam Ranh; and Can Tho and Vung Tau from Saigon. This was the concept that was developed in the summer and early fall of 1965. Before the end of the year, however, it became increasingly obvious that Qui Nhon should become a fourth deep-draft port with full pier accommodations, since Qui Nhon had become the most logical point from which to support extensive operations in the highlands. (*Map 4*) Cam Ranh Bay became less important for direct support of ground operations, but it developed into a theater depot and an intertheater air terminal. These four deep-draft ports—Da Nang, Qui Nhon, Cam Ranh Bay, and Saigon—became the keystones of the base development plan and the centers of what eventually became semiautonomous logistical enclaves.

Once the concept of these sustaining ports was established, the program of base development proceeded in logical order. While deep-draft piers were being provided and channels to the piers were being dredged, each port area was to be expanded to include depot facilities for storage and further distribution of petroleum products, ammunition, rations, equipment, and a myriad of other materials. Provisions were made in each port area complex for the essential supporting services: maintenance, supply, transportation, hospitalization, communications, and personnel accommodations.

It logically followed that major air bases should also be developed in each principal port area, mainly because there was a need for high-capacity port facilities to satisfy aircraft demands for petroleum and ammunition. To facilitate the air delivery of critical supplies, material was quickly shuffled from dockside to waiting aircraft.

At Da Nang the existing air base was expanded with an additional runway, aprons, and cargo handling facilities. A new fighter-bomber base was constructed near Qui Nhon at Phu Cat in II Corps. A fighter-bomber and logistics terminal was built at Cam Ranh Bay, and at Saigon both Tan Son Nhut and Bien Hoa were upgraded and expanded with parallel runways. Major tactical or logistical air bases were also constructed at the shallow-draft ports of Chu Lai in I Corps and Phan Rang in II Corps, which were the satellite ports of Da Nang and Cam Ranh. Not included in the

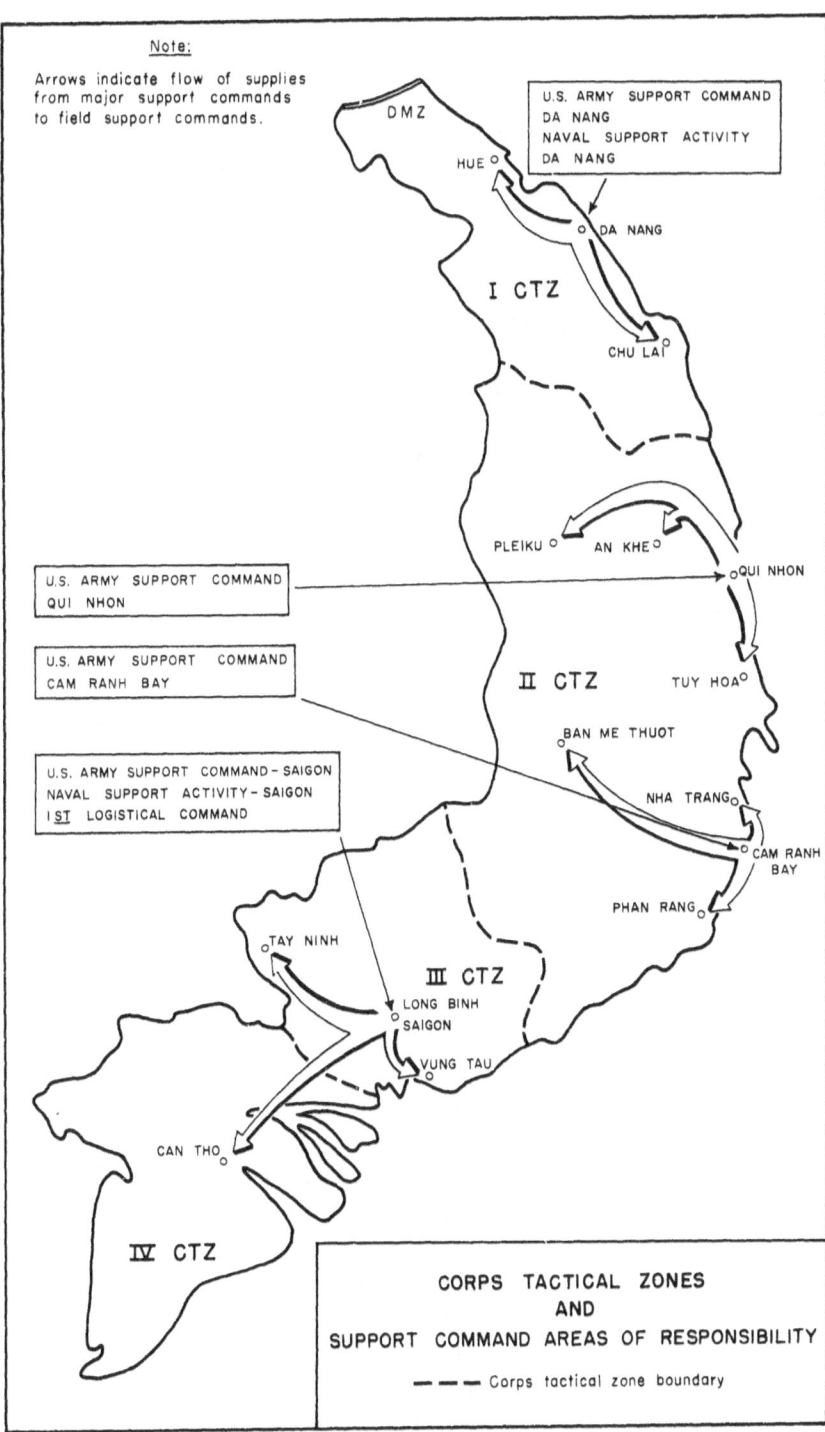

MAP 4

original base development concept was the air base at Tuy Hoa in central II Corps, which was established by late 1966 with its supporting single-pier deep-draft port at Vung Ro.

Operations of the major depot complexes were extended through forward operating elements. The ultimate effect of this matrix of primary logistical port-depot complexes and satellite forward displacements was to create an extensive logistics support grid. On short notice logistical support could be provided to any tactical element by "plugging in" to the grid.

The construction program to support American and allied forces in South Vietnam did not evolve from any single planning action; it developed from immediate requirements in 1965 and continued to expand as needs increased. The underdeveloped nature of Vietnam and the lack of available base facilities placed a premium on a rapid construction program. The initial operations plan directed the U.S. Army, Ryukyu Islands, to provide base development plans for Army forces designated for deployment to Vietnam. The plans that were developed were adequate, since they were responsive to operational requirements and were detailed enough so that the type and scope of facilities needed could be identified. The real problem, however, was that the plans were written for a force of 64,000 men, whereas the accelerated troop buildup led to a force totaling 81,000 in July 1965 and 184,000 by December 1965. The engineer staffs of the Commander in Chief, Pacific, the Military Assistance Command, Vietnam, and subordinate elements were inadequately manned for the prompt development of the plans necessary to meet the force buildup. Therefore, not only the development of but the planning for base facilities was concurrent with the rapid increase in force structure. It was clear from the beginning that certain functional types of facilities would be required, but the quantities and locations were not known. The construction program changed with each change in operational and logistical concepts and requirements. Not until the end of 1966 was the program sufficiently clear to identify these principal requirements:

1. 8 jet fighter bases with 10,000-foot runways
2. 6 new deepwater ports with 28 deep-draft berths
3. 26 hospitals with 8,280 beds
4. 280,000 kilowatts of electrical power
5. 10.4 million square feet of warehousing
6. 3.1 million barrels of POL storage
7. 5,460,000 square feet of ammunition storage
8. 75 new C-130 airfields
9. $27.1 million of communication facilities

PLANNING AND THE CONSTRUCTION CONCEPT

10. 39 million cubic meters of dredging
11. 4,100 kilometers of highway
12. 434,000 acres of land clearing
13. 182 wells for water

At MACV headquarters, before February 1966, responsibilities pertaining to base development planning and construction priorities were inhibited by the inability of the limited engineer staff to handle a program of the magnitude required to meet operational needs. Consequently, priorities for projects or complexes were often resolved at General Westmoreland's level.

Requirements for construction were generally developed at the base installation level and processed in the country through the service chain of command. At different levels the requests were reviewed for validity and integrated into a composite priority listing according to individual service needs subject to corps tactical zone co-ordination.

Appropriate command interest at all levels was evidenced by the successful accomplishment of the construction program despite extreme difficulties. Integration of operational and support planning was after early 1966 probably more complete than in any previous conflict. The personal interest and action of commanders, both tactical and engineer, overcame the complexity of multiple chains of command and the relatively restrictive funding procedures in effect. The Secretary of Defense's decision to have a director of construction co-ordinate the entire construction program was a critical factor in its over-all success.

Still, local commanders' interests normally focused on projects which bore directly on their operations. Those which supported other agencies were slighted. Local commanders generally tended to upgrade priority designators excessively to get higher priorities for their own projects on the integrated construction schedule, allocation of materials and equipment, construction standards, and rate of progress. Such actions ultimately worked to the detriment of other projects, which in some cases had higher legitimate priorities.

For all of these projects, planning called for austerity. Although rigid control prevailed in the early days of the troop buildup, it became more relaxed as the situation changed. Minimum essential requirements were originally provided which allowed only the minimum facilities an arriving or relocating unit needed to occupy a new location on a temporary basis. Authorization was limited to concrete slabs for mess hall tents, grading and stabilization necessary to erect unframed tentage, stabilized parking areas for TOE equipment and aircraft, minimum open storage, area drainage, access and primary roads, culverts, field showers, burn-out latrines, and revetments for aircraft. The minimum requirements were also the result of a shortage of skilled support troops.

President Johnson's decision in November 1965 not to order a general call-up of Reserve and National Guard units imposed a major restraint on the deployment of sufficient numbers of engineer construction troops to Vietnam. The National Guard and the Reserves contained the majority of troop construction units. This problem, along with the lack of a skilled local population, increased our reliance on civilian contractors for major construction in the combat area. Consequently, the contractor construction capability already in Vietnam had to be expanded. The magnitude of the contractor effort became so vast and diversified that it could correctly be termed a construction industry. The peak strength of the contractors' work force, attained in mid-1966, was 51,044 personnel, of which less than 10 percent were American. (*Chart 5*)

In general, the contractor was given the larger, more complicated jobs in relatively secure areas, while troops concentrated on work in forward areas. But there was no sharp division between work assigned to contractors or troops. In a number of instances, contractors and engineer troops worked together. There were times when contractors were not available and projects had to be turned over to engineer troops units. At other times, troops were needed

CHART 5—MANPOWER

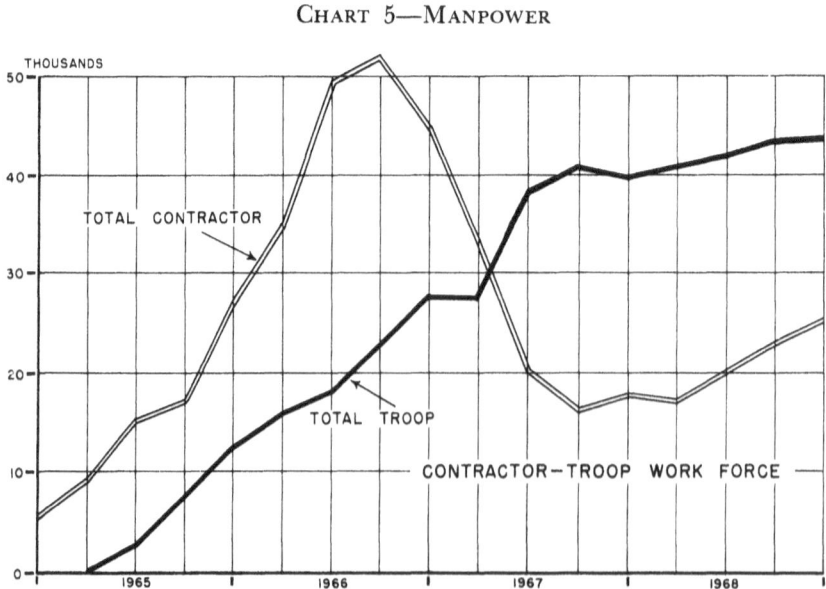

PLANNING AND THE CONSTRUCTION CONCEPT   43

to support tactical operations and their projects had to be left to contractors.

With rising construction needs and costs, both Congress and Secretary McNamara became closely involved in construction control. On 3 September 1965 an assistant for construction operations was established within the Office of the Deputy Assistant Secretary of Defense for Installations and Housing, OASD (I&L). Its staff consisted of one officer in the grade of O-6 from each service under the command of a general officer, the first of whom was Brigadier General Charles C. Noble, U.S. Army. His essential duties were to monitor the military construction programs, and support them before Congress, to assure that they were proceeding on schedule, and that any obstacles were identified and removed. With control points established at MACV in Vietnam and in OASD (I&L), the Secretary of Defense was in a position to deal directly and on a day-to-day basis with construction matters involving MACV, elements of his own office, and Congress. The Secretary of Defense prescribed detailed procedures covering such matters as construction standards; procedures for review, authorization, and changes in programs; construction status and forecast reports; and MACV construction directives.

On 21 December 1967, the two Army engineer brigades in Vietnam were denied authority to issue construction directives which exceeded the scope of Engineer Command directives already published. Before this date engineer brigade and group commanders operated under a rather liberal policy which allowed them to initiate construction that in their judgment was necessary within the scope of general directives issued by MACV and USARV. Once such a project was started, the engineer commander involved would simply request the Engineer Command to issue a construction directive to cover the project. One of the problems with this procedure was that it gave the USARV staff no opportunity to evaluate the requirement in light of the over-all military situation, the total construction program, or the priorities before work began. As a result, engineer commanders occasionally found that units for which they were building a cantonment had been relocated, or were scheduled to relocate. Earlier, there were always new units coming in to occupy the unused space, but by late 1967 the situation changed. All commanders became concerned with overbuilding and were careful to stay within authorized construction limits. The practice was to apply minimum essential standards.

There were no set construction standards at the beginning of the program except limitations on living space and the general admonition that facilities would be minimum and austere. Standards evolved slowly and were inconsistent. Theater standards were finally developed and accepted to minimize costs based on duration of occupancy and construction time. The factors which played a major role in determining standards were the mission of the unit for which facilities were provided, the permanency of units in a given location, and the philosophy of each military service.

The problems of establishing standards in Vietnam were complicated by variations in philosophies as well as by characteristics peculiar to the war. Both Army and Marine Corps ground combat units traditionally have been equipped and trained to operate in the field with minimum facilities. Still, there were a great many differences of opinion concerning standards that would be used in the construction of division and brigade base camps. With advanced types of jet aircraft, more sophisticated technical equipment became necessary at air base sites. Consequently, fixed bases, as opposed to expeditionary flying fields from which Air Force and Marine tactical fighter units had previously operated, became sophisticated industrial centers with facilities constructed to relatively high standards.

The rise in cantonment standards came into being because combat operations were conducted and supported from relatively static base camps and logistical facilities. The upshot was a degree of refinement and a higher standard of living for support troops (and in some situations for combat troops) than in any other war in our nation's history. This rise in standards had a major impact on construction requirements. For example, the almost complete elimination of B rations and the large-scale use of frozen foods, fresh fruits and vegetables, and dairy products created increased requirements for cold storage facilities, which thus greatly exceeded planning factors for refrigeration units based on previous experience.

The tropical climate justified air conditioning for specific cantonment areas such as administrative and planning areas; certain medical facilities; and quarters for night-flying aircraft pilots, senior officers, and civilian personnel. This was not envisioned in the initial planning, and considerable time elapsed before a policy was formulated and enforced. Still other delays were experienced in completing facilities because of the long lead time required to procure and ship this sophisticated equipment to Vietnam.

To combat inflation in the country by absorbing dollars, the service exchanges marketed a variety of household items never before available in a theater of operations. Many items not available directly from the exchanges could be ordered by mail from home or mail-order houses. Consequently, television sets, room-size air conditioners, electric fans, hot plates, small refrigerators, toasters, and electric percolators became commonplace in many living quar-

TABLE 1—CONSTRUCTION STANDARDS

Facility	Temporary	Intermediate	Field
Troop housing	Austere wood buildings; 1- and 2-story barracks	Austere wood huts; tents with wood frame and floors	Austere wood huts; Class IV tents with wood frames and floors
Mess hall	Pre-engineered metal or wood building	Pre-engineered metal or wood building	Wood building; tents
Dispensary	Pre-engineered metal or wood building	Pre-engineered metal or wood building	Wood building; tents
Electricity	Central power and distribution	Nontactical generators	Nontactical generators; TOE generators
Water supply	Piped water distribution	Point supply with limited distribution	Point supply
Sewage	Waterborne	Consolidated treatment; burn-out latrines	Burn-out latrines
Roads	Paved	Stabilized	Dirt

ters. The resultant unprecedented requirements for eletcrical power necessitated procurement of electrical generators and the design or redesign of electrical distribution systems heretofore unknown in war.

On 4 June 1964 General Westmoreland published a directive which assigned responsibility for construction standards to the Deputy Officer in Charge of Construction, Southeast Asia, and published the first general guidelines for such standards. (*Table 1*) After several changes, an October 1966 revision to this directive prescribed three cantonment standards based on expected tenure of occupancy. These standards, which with minor modification were to prevail for the remainder of the conflict, were as follows:

Field: Category C—Cantonments for forces whose activities are such that they may be characterized as essentially transient. Occupancy less than two years. (Wood floors, tents, dirt roads, minimum essential requirement latrine facilities, and minimum utilities.)

Intermediate: Category B—Cantonments for forces subject to move at infrequent intervals. Anticipated duration of occupancy: 24–48 months. (Wood or concrete floors with tent frames, roofs, some paved roads, full electrical utilities, and minimum requirements for latrine facilities.)

Temporary: Category A—Cantonments for forces not expected to move in the foreseeable future. Occupancy over forty-eight months.

An annex to the regulation prescribed these standards for various types of facilities and provided for exceptions when approved by General Westmoreland.

Inasmuch as initial requirements for facilities were programed through separate service channels, different service philosophies were reflected in early requests to Congress. Congress approved program funds based on these philosophies. Once under construction, however, wide variations became very apparent, and considerable dissatisfaction arose among the troops, particularly those returning from the field. Initial attempts at standardization had the effect of lowering the standards of the Air Force and the Navy and raising those of the Army and the Marine Corps. As might be expected, these attempts were only partially successful.

It also became apparent that the permanency of a camp, particularly in areas where troop density was high, necessitated higher standards for water and sewer systems. The life expectancy of a facility or complex was also pertinent. The question was whether to build for one, five, or ten years. The degree of permanency had a major impact on maintenance and continuing operating costs.

The standards finally promulgated by General Westmoreland in October 1966 were believed to be sound in concept and broad enough to cover all requirement combinations of mission, permanency, and service philosophies. There was difficulty, however, in determining the standards of construction authorized for the base camp, because the base population varied in degrees of permanency. This was especially true in the major depot complexes and in division base camps.

In application of these standards, a basic decision was required to determine the maximum level of comfort to be permitted and supported in the theater. In Vietnam "temporary" buildings were in many respects comparable in standards to mobilization structures built in the United States during World War II and still in use. Authorizing these standards in Vietnam meant that costs would average on the order of $3,000 per man.

The degree of permanency, once decided upon, would control uniformity in construction standards for all facilities in an area regardless of service component. Ports, depots, air bases, and major hospitals would all have the same or similar standards. However, an example of the disparity in standards was the authorization of 1.5 kilowatts of electrical power per man at major bases. Although the industrial needs at air bases accounted for some differences, at most other facilities the standard was 0.7 kilowatts per man regardless of base requirements. Consequently, there was inadequate power at many Army facilities.

During and following World War II, the Navy had faced similar base building problems and had developed the Advanced Base Functional Component System (ABFCS). During the buildup in Vietnam, the Navy used many elements of that system. The Da Nang hospital was constructed almost entirely of quonset huts, which make up a large part of the system. However, the standards of the ABFCS were quite austere.

The Army's functional components system for base building was different from the Navy's concept. The Engineer Functional Components System (EFCS) consisted of data published in three technical manuals, TM 5–301, 5–302, and 5–303, which provided staff guidance, site and structure layout plans, construction details, and bills of matériel for the construction of buildings and facilities in the theater of operations.

The EFCS was based on a building-block concept and made up of items, equipages, and installations that could be combined as required to provide necessary facilities. The EFCS was intended as a basic planning guide for the construction of facilities in the theater of operations, and it was used to order approximately two-thirds of the construction matériel for Army troop construction programs. However, the EFCS proved to be unsatisfactory and its use was discontinued, because many required facilities were not included in the system, and the design criteria provided were not compatible with Vietnam requirements.

Unlike as in World War II and the Korean War, funding of base development in Vietnam was arranged through what is technically known as Military Construction, Army (MCA), which made use of mainly peacetime programing and budgetary procedures.

During earlier wars, worldwide construction and procurement of matériel for engineer troops were funded from the appropriation called Engineer Service, Army. Funding was in the nature of a bulk allotment and was not limited by authorization or appropriations for specific items or locations. This system was discontinued in fiscal year 1953. Since then procurement of matériel has been funded from the new Operations and Maintenance appropriation.

It was this fund that was used to a small extent for base construction in Vietnam, but its authority only provided for new construction projects with funded costs of less than $25,000 each or for maintenance and repairs of existing projects in larger amounts.

Whereas the Engineer Service, Army, and Operations and Maintenance funds permitted considerable flexibility, the military construction appropriation is extremely rigid and unsuited for rapidly changing conditions in the combat zone. The appropriation involves an orderly system which has evolved over the years to satisfy peacetime construction requirements. It requires complete construction plans and specifications and involves maximum visibility and tight controls to assure that the programs are followed. It provides for annual authorization and fundings for specific projects or line items and identified by locations or installations. Until 15 October 1966 the appropriation was also used to undertake urgent minor construction projects in Vietnam not exceeding $200,000 and those up to a maximum aggregate value of $10 million per year.

Normally the appropriation cycle takes three years for complete development. After programing, budgeting, and Congressional action, the authority to spend is established and finally construction may begin. This cyclic approach has built-in delays which, while not especially a handicap to peacetime construction in the United States, were extremely troublesome in Vietnam.

In a combat area, time is of the essence. Construction programing and scheduling in Vietnam were upset by a number of factors—changes in operational plans, force levels, troop deployments and redeployments, enemy activity, soil conditions, site relocations, weather, and the availability of shipping. A paper work marathon ensued whenever a project was changed or introduced.

Congress and the Secretary of Defense agreed to certain modifications to adapt the system for support of operations in Vietnam. Requirements were incorporated in a separate Title of Authorization Act in which requirements of all three services were presented as a joint-requirements package. Authorization was requested of, and granted by, Congress as a lump-sum amount for each service in each act in order to provide maximum flexibility in spending.

The basis for each lump-sum authorization was a specific list of estimated requirements in terms of broad categories of facilities such as airfields, ports, hospitals, highways, and troop housing—all by locations. General Westmoreland was permitted to increase the amount of any account by up to 10 percent as long as the sum total of the over-all program was not exceeded. New procedures adopted in early 1967 doubled the number of categories and expanded the number of locations. Inasmuch as many separate projects had to be listed, this system was too complex, involved too many people, and generated far too much paper for anyone's benefit. However, this new 1967 system was made to work.

Some difficulty was experienced in convincing everyone concerned of the continuing need for reprograming flexibility, particularly from mid-1966 on. In his instructions of February 1966, Secretary McNamara had permitted General Westmoreland to transfer program authorities without advance approval from one category to another, provided that funding allocated to a category was not increased by more than 10 percent. This degree of money shuffling was considered rather handy, because the 10 percent applied to categories which were rather large, such as cantonments, which in the 1966 supplemental appropriation was funded at $77.7 million. As time passed flexibility was reduced. Instead of the sixteen broad functional facility categories originally authorized, a conversion to the more numerous standard Defense Department facility categories was directed in January 1967. Starting with the 1967 Supplemental Program, a project had to be within the scope of work cited on a DD Form 1391, which closely paralleled the normal peacetime station listing of line items. The Commander, Military Assistance Command, retained project adjustment authority up to the larger of $50,000 or 10 percent of the facility category at a given location. Greater adjustments entailed OSD approval and included notification of Congress for adjustments exceeding $1 million.

Funding for Army construction in Vietnam was provided through a series of regular, supplemental, reprograming, and emergency appropriations starting in fiscal year 1965. A list of appropriations for the fiscal years 1965–69 follows (*Table 2*):

TABLE 2—CONSTRUCTION APPROPRIATIONS

Fiscal Year	Type Appropriation	In Thousands
1965	Regular	$ 15,454
1965	Supplemental	36,060
1966	Regular	30,189
1966	Amendment	35,942
1966	Supplemental	285,900
1966	Transfer, including MAP	138,386
1967	Supplemental	217,556
1968	Regular	31,424
1968	Contingency transfer	39,600
1968	Supplemental	16,400
1969	Regular	96,683
Total		$943,594

CHAPTER V

The Bases

The port of Saigon and, to a lesser extent, the port of Cam Ranh Bay were the only harbors in South Vietnam capable of docking deep-draft oceangoing vessels before the force buildup in early 1965. There were shallow-draft port facilities at Nha Trang, Qui Nhon, and Da Nang, and there were numerous beaches along the coast over which cargo could be landed from ships lying offshore. But in 1965 only one berth in the old port of Saigon was permanently allotted to American forces, although from two to ten were used at various times. In January 1966 three berths were permanently assigned for United States military use in Saigon. Cam Ranh Bay had at that time only one deep-draft pier in operation which was insufficient for existing and projected cargo handling requirements.

From Washington a close watch was being kept on the operation of Vietnamese ports throughout 1965 and 1966. Ninety percent of all military supplies and equipment were destined to arrive in Vietnam by deep-draft vessels, and millions of tons of foodstuffs and nation-building equipment imported by the U.S. Agency for International Development and the Vietnamese government were at the same time competing for berth space at the port of Saigon. Until an effective Pacific theater movement agency was in operation to balance port reception capability with inbound shipping and until limits were placed on out-of-country cargo shippers, a tremendous backlog of vessels could be expected in Vietnamese waters or in nearby port facilities. At one time over 100 deep-draft vessels were awaiting discharge in Vietnamese waters or were in holding areas at Okinawa in the Ryukyus or Subic Bay in the Philippines. Many ships loaded with supplies had to wait several months for berthing and off-loading.

The Army lacked the shallow-draft shipping necessary to take advantage of shallow port facilities, but this was offset somewhat by landing cargo across undeveloped beaches; deep-draft vessels were unloaded into Army and Navy landing craft and civilian barges. Although supplies could be landed this way, it was not sufficiently

EARLY CONSTRUCTION at *Cam Ranh Bay by the 497th Port Construction Company.*

rapid and would certainly not work as supplies were increased. There never really were enough lighters or barges.

The 1st Logistical Command Engineer Section was responsible for initial construction planning for Army requirements in Vietnam, including the development of port facilities. This small section began the initial development of ports. Upon the arrival of the 18th Engineer Brigade and with the organization of a USARV Engineer Section, this responsibility was transferred to a new headquarters. Planning for the over-all development of ports within Vietnam became the responsibility of the Assistant Chief of Staff for Logistics, the MACV J–4.

Later in the summer of 1965, the USARV Engineer Section made studies of required construction to refine the original plans. The only organized Army port construction company, the 497th, arrived at Cam Ranh Bay late that summer from Fort Belvoir, Virginia, to assist in the port construction program. The 497th helped develop requirements and plans for both long- and short-range port facilities throughout Vietnam, exclusive of the I Corps area, whose development remained with the Navy.

The plan was to develop Saigon, Da Nang, and Cam Ranh Bay into major logistical bases and Qui Nhon, Nha Trang, Phan Rang, Chu Lai, Phu Bai, and Vung Tau into minor support bases. Because of the tactical and geographical isolation of these ports, all supplies had to come by sea. Port development involved more than the construction of additional piers. Barge off-loading facilities, ramps for landing craft, and petroleum unloading facilities were all required.

To begin the port construction projects, a fleet of dredges was assembled under the flag of the Navy's Officer In Charge of Construction. The hydraulic dredge is without question the most useful piece of equipment afloat for harbor and channel projects, reclamation and landfill, and for providing the huge stockpiles of sand necessary for other construction projects. In 1966 the dredge fleet included two side-casting and three hopper dredges, the *Davison* and the *Hyde* from the Army Corps of Engineers civil works fleet, and eighteen pipeline cutterhead dredges. During the period November 1965 through May 1970, hydraulic dredges excavated 64.8 million cubic meters of canal, entrance channel, and river bottom material.

The scope of work, availability of funds, hydrographic surveys, soils explorations, length of maintenance and overhaul periods, and desired completion dates are as in the planning and executings of dredging operations as in any other engineering project; but familiar problems were compounded by a few others in Vietnam. For example, the monsoon season interrupted earthwork on land reclamation projects; civilian crews operating dredges had to be protected against enemy attack; safety measures were imperative for dredging in areas where the marine bottom was peppered with live explosives; and the extremely long supply line was encumbered with faulty requisition transmission, frustrating concepts, and an extreme shortage of needed replacement parts. Added to this was an ever-changing tactical situation which would not respect previously established readiness dates or work schedules.

Site acquisition was the first step in hydraulic fill operations. Maintenance dredging projects usually encountered little opposition, since both the military and civilians considered land reclamation beneficial. However, when improved land was required for a project, time-consuming negotiations followed. Requests for hydraulic fill projects had to be forwarded by the military to the Interior Ministerial Real Estate Committee, Ministry of Defense, Government of Vietnam. If approved, IMREC directed the appropriate province chief to form a committee to evaluate real-estate costs and to determine what homes, graves, facilities, or other improvements would require relocation and to whom compensation would be paid. After the site was acquired, actual work could begin. To illustrate how dredging operations progressed in Vietnam, we can consider one project—at Dong Tam in IV Corps.

Dong Tam, a marshy area lying along the My Tho River, eight kilometers west of the town of My Tho and sixty-five kilometers southwest of Saigon, was selected as the site for a joint Army-Navy military complex. To develop the location into a base required excavating a rice paddy for development into a turning basin and dredging an entrance channel into the basin from the My Tho River. The over-all plan also called for dredging sand from the river, creating a landfill of one square mile and providing a stockpile for airfield, concrete, and road construction projects in the surrounding area. The 16-inch pipeline cutterhead, *Cho Gao*, first of five dredges assigned, started work on 4 August 1966. The basin and channel had a higher priority than the sand stockpile and were completed in April 1967. The shortage of sand at Dong Tam persisted.

Dredging at Dong Tam was not without combat losses. First, the *Jamaica Bay*, a 30-inch pipeline cutterhead dredge, was sunk by sappers on 9 January 1967. Two American crew members were drowned during the incident. Subsequently, the dredge was salvaged, but while under tow off the port of Vung Tau, she encountered heavy seas and sank. Attempts to raise her were unsuccessful and the dredge now lies on the bottom of the South China Sea off the coast of South Vietnam. Fortunately her sister dredge, the *New Jersey*, was also in the country and available as a replacement.

The *Thu Bon I*, a 12-inch pipeline cutterhead dredge, was sunk by sappers on 28 July 1968 while working in the entrance channel. Following salvage, a survey team estimated that repair costs would reach at least 75 percent of the purchase price; therefore, the decision was made to scrap the dredge for parts. She was replaced by a similar 12-inch dredge, the *Thu Bon II*. Thirteen months later, on 22 September 1969, the U.S. Navy-owned 27-inch pipeline cutterhead *Sandpumper* sucked up live ordnance from the bottom of the My Tho River and sank following detonation of the explosive. For a period of four months, attempts were made to raise her but, as in the case of the *Thu Bon I*, a cost survey revealed that salvage and repair were not economically feasible. A disposition board recommended that the dredge be stricken from the register of U.S. Navy vessels and turned over to military authorities for disposal. The

Sandpumper now rests in the My Tho River, posing no immediate threat to navigation and awaiting her ultimate fate.

Finally, on 22 November 1969, sappers sank the 30-inch pipeline cutterhead *New Jersey*. Harbor Clearance Unit One, a U.S. Navy team from the Subic Bay Naval Base, raised her on 30 December. Taken to Singapore in January 1970, she underwent overhaul and repairs in the Keppel Yards. In May 1970 she was towed back to Vietnam, refitted with the gear that had not been taken to Singapore, and put back in operation performing maintenance dredging at Qui Nhon.

An outstanding contribution in expediting the port construction program was made by using DeLong Floating Piers. These patented products of the DeLong Corporation are sectional and can be fabricated outside of the theater of operations in a variety of sizes and configurations, towed to a site, and quickly emplaced. These piers made it possible to develop additional deep-draft ports and berths at Qui Nhon, Vung Tau, Cam Ranh Bay, Vung Ro, and Da Nang in record time.

The first DeLong pier with all its equipment and spare parts was towed to Cam Ranh Bay from the east coast of the United

A DELONG PIER *under construction at the Cam Ranh port facility.*

States in a trip that took about two months. The men of the 497th Port Construction Company, who were to place the pier, were inexperienced in the construction of DeLongs and had to learn on the job. Advice and technical assistance were provided by representatives of the manufacturer.

The first pier was essentially a 90x300-foot barge supported by eighteen tubular steel caissons six feet in diameter and fifty feet long. The additional caisson sections were joined end to end to provide the required length. Collars attached to the pier caissons were driven into the harbor bottom, and pneumatic jacks, which were a part of the collars, were then used to jack the barge up on its legs to a usable height.

Before placing the pier, no test piles could be driven or test bores taken because the equipment was lacking. Test bore data was available for the adjacent pier, but the depth of refusal for the caissons could not be accurately predicted. Because of a mud layer beneath the sand bottom of the bay, three lengths of caisson 150 feet long were required at each location. Although two sections could be joined before erection, the third had to be welded on in place, a process that required twenty days. The first DeLong pier, completed in mid-December 1965, doubled the capacity of the Cam Ranh Bay port. This pier required forty-five days for construction by sixteen men. Engineers estimated that a timber-pile pier would have required at least six months' work by a construction platoon of forty men, plus supporting equipment and operators, as well as a large number of hard to get timber piles and construction timber. It was demonstrated that significant savings in time and material could be had with the DeLong pier compared to an equivalent timber-pile pier.

The two existing piers for deep-draft vessels still lacked in-transit storage areas, so a sheet-pile bulkhead was constructed between the causeways to each pier. The area behind the bulkhead was filled in using a 30-inch pipeline dredge and 96,000 cubic yards of material. The surface was then stabilized to provide a large cargo-handling area. *(Map 5)*

Work started on the third general cargo pier at Cam Ranh Bay in May 1966. This was a two-barge DeLong pier ninety feet wide by six hundred feet long. It was installed by the DeLong Corporation, which was under contract to the Army to install all the additional DeLong piers used in Vietnam, with engineer units providing connecting causeways, abutments, roads, and hardstands.

In September 1965, large-scale landing ship, tank (LST), operations began. LST's transported supplies from Saigon, Cam Ranh Bay, and Okinawa to the shallow ports of Qui Nhon, Vung Tau,

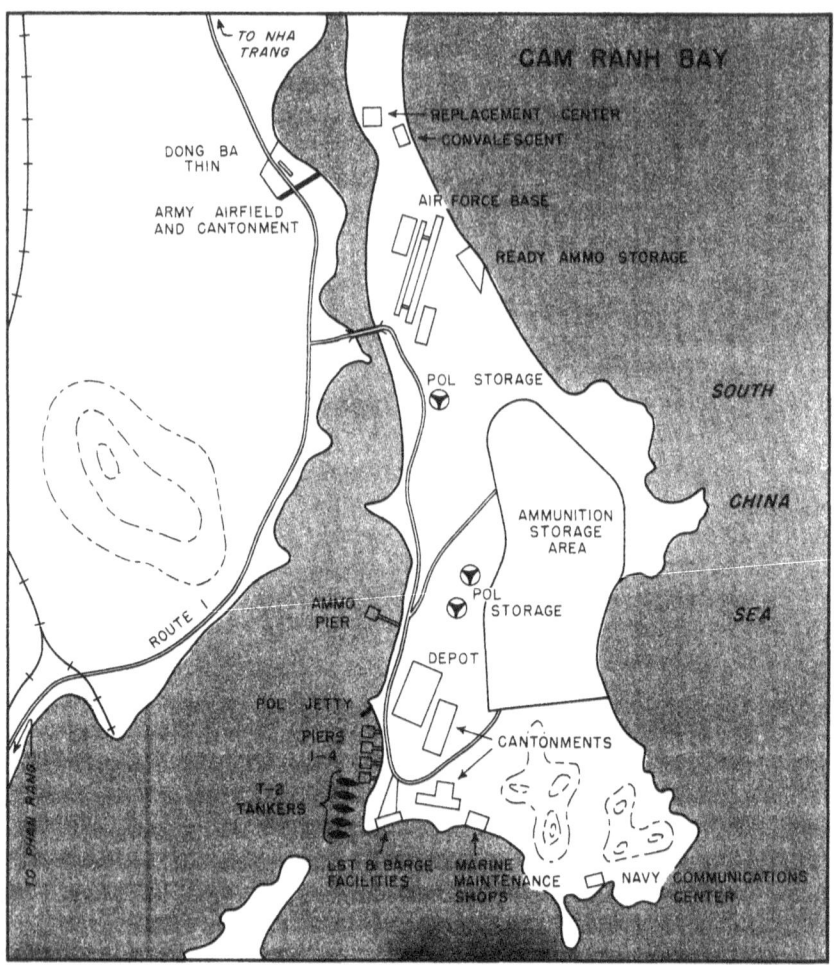

MAP 5

and Nha Trang. Consequently, the first job for the port construction company was to increase the traffic-handling capacity at these sites.

Sand on many Vietnamese beaches becomes almost impassable with heavy use and severely limits the loads that can be transported across the beach. Many methods of stabilizing sand were tried unsuccessfully, and wave action over the beaches washed away most expedients. However, late in 1965, large coral beds were found offshore at Cam Ranh Bay; these deposits were then blasted and excavated with draglines. The coral was crushed and hauled to the landing sites. The foreshore area between high and low tide marks was excavated to eighteen inches, and the crushed coral was placed

First DeLong *in use at Cam Ranh.*

in layers and compacted with rollers, then the beach was graded to its original alignment. This process gave satisfactory results that lasted for several months with only minor repairs.

At Cam Ranh Bay the first expeditionary airfield was under construction by Raymond, Morrison-Knudsen, and the first jet fighter aircraft were scheduled to arrive on 1 November 1965. However, the fuel supply available was inadequate, so in early October work started on a 400-foot timber fuel jetty extending out to the five and a half fathom line. The floating pile-driving equipment of the port construction company was used to construct the jetty, and on 1 November fuel was being pumped from a tanker to the Cam Ranh Bay Air Base ten miles away. But marine wood borers, which are prevalent in Vietnamese waters, caused a goodly amount of damage to the jetty's untreated timbers within a very short time. Treated timbers were not available for bracing of either the POL jetty or the wharf, and lateral and longitudinal bracing had to be replaced quite often.

With the addition of the third and fourth DeLong piers, and more than 3,000 linear feet of bulkhead, the port facility formed a major part of the logistical area at Cam Ranh Bay, which became one of the largest in the Republic of Vietnam.

Soon after arriving in Cam Ranh Bay, the 1st Platoon of the 497th Engineer Company went to Qui Nhon where with elements of the 84th Engineer Battalion a considerable effort was being made to increase the capacity of port facilities. A "Navy cube" floating pier, 42 feet wide by 192 feet long, was built and connected to the shore with a 200-foot rock-filled causeway in February 1966. These cube piers consisting of 5x7x7-foot cubes of steel fastened together with angle irons and cables were used extensively in Vietnam. They could be towed for short distances and emplaced where needed, requiring very little on-site construction time.

Inasmuch as Qui Nhon was a shallow-draft port, ramps for landing craft were needed. However, no suitable land was available. The first step, therefore, was the extension of the Qui Nhon Peninsula with approximately 45,000 cubic yards of fill to create a usable area measuring 620 feet by 360 feet. A sheet-pile cofferdam was built to exclude water from the work site, and select fill was placed and faced with riprap, or a lose stone foundation, on a slope of five to one. This extension to the peninsula provided an excellent place for LCU's (landing craft, utility) and LCM's (landing craft, mechanized) to unload and also increased the in-transit storage area by more than 100 percent. (*Map 6*)

In February 1966 Qui Nhon was changed from a support area to a logistical base, which required increased storage capacity. Ton-

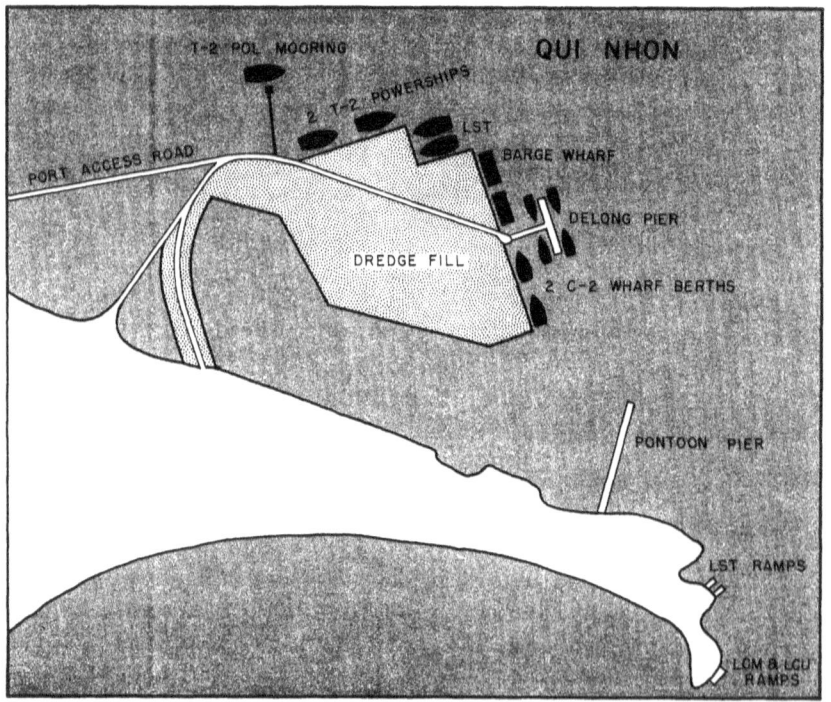

MAP 6

nage requirements were calculated, and the design for the port was developed. Phase I included eight barge unloading points, four deep-draft berths provided by DeLong piers, and two permanent LST ramps. In June 1966 the 937th Engineer Group began building a four-lane port access road 1.5 miles across the bay to bypass the congested city of Qui Nhon. The subbase of the access road was hydraulic fill. The approach channel, some two miles in length, and the turning basin were dredged. A total of 4,000,000 cubic yards of material was moved. A submarine pipeline for the transfer of petroleum from tankers to tank farms was installed. Two 4-inch lines near the landing craft ramps and one 4-inch line on the seaward side of Qui Nhon were also put in but were accessible only to small tankers. For stabilizing the tankers while unloading, a system of anchorage and breasting dolphins was rigged at the sea end of the pipelines.

With the increased movement of troops into the Saigon area, the deep-draft facilities there proved completely inadequate. However, a plan was already under way to construct a new port on the Saigon River upstream from the city. The location was chosen by Captain Maury Werth, U.S. Navy, who was a special assistant to the MACV J–4. This site, called Newport, was in a sparsely populated area adjacent to a main highway connecting Saigon with the newly developing Long Binh area some twenty miles from Saigon. This massive project financed by the Army was constructed by RMK–BRJ.

To meet the immediate need for additional port facilities in the Saigon area, the 18th Engineer Brigade built six cargo barge unloading points near the Long Binh Depot. The ammunition unloading points were constructed on the Dong Nai River at Cogido, and two piers were constructed for docking.

The 536th Port Construction Detachment, consisting of a construction platoon and construction support elements, operated in Vung Tau during the spring of 1966. This detachment developed temporary LST facilities, timber-pile piers, sheet-pile bulkheads, and DeLong pier abutments.

Improvements in the flow of cargo not only had a military impact but also aided the Vietnamese people, since a steady flow of consumer goods helped to combat the inflation which threatened to ruin the Vietnamese economy. To a very great extent, the success in providing logistical support to American forces in South Vietnam was a direct result of port expansion.

The capacity of permanent port facilities in South Vietnam increased many times over, with the construction of new facilities at Newport, Saigon, Vung Tau, Cam Ranh Bay, Qui Nhon, Da

Nang, and other installations. Port development throughout the coastal region of South Vietnam gave the republic permanent access to the sea, thus promoting development of a stabilized economy and the emergence of Vietnam as an Asian trading center. (*Map 7*)

As the building of improved ports and docking facilities continued, a network of air bases was under construction which further

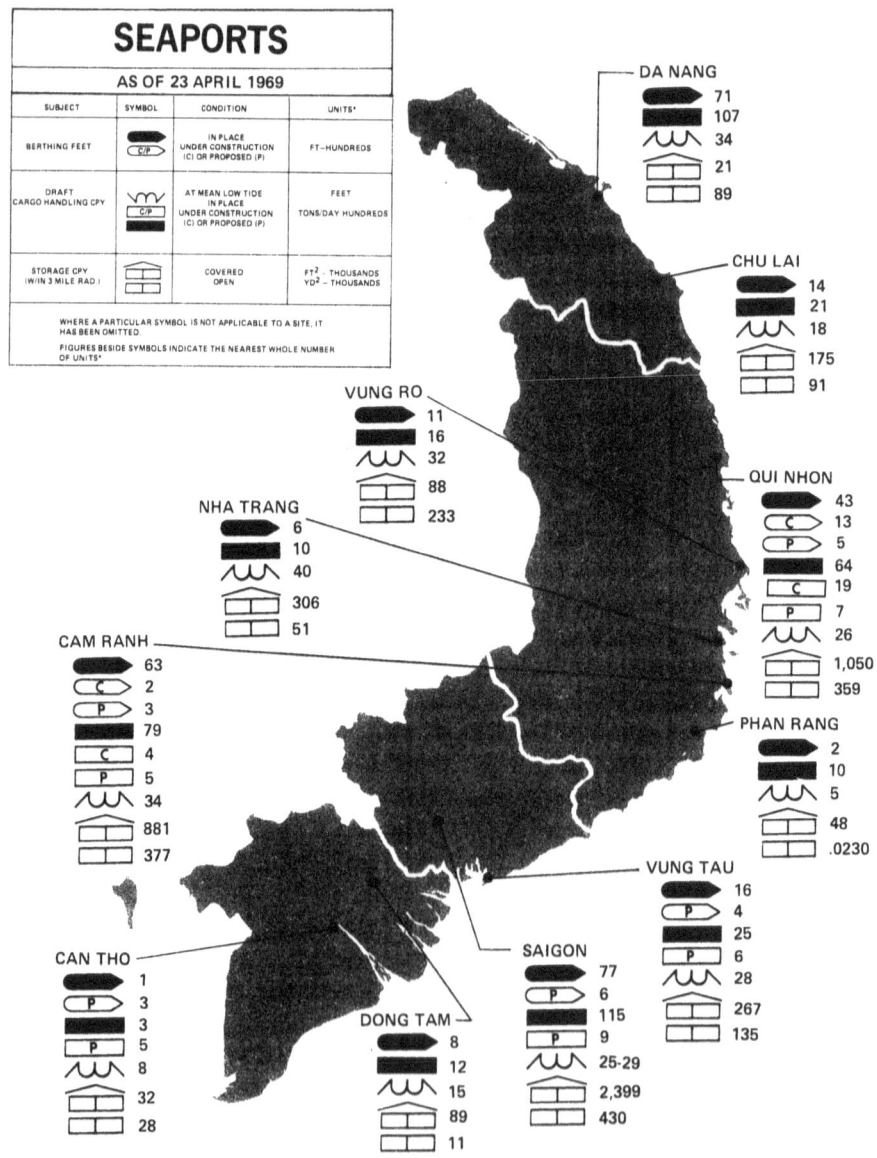

MAP 7

absorbed the engineers' attention. The differences in high-performance aircraft used by the French and Vietnamese, as opposed to the American military machine, forecasted the development of jet air bases in Vietnam that would be an engineering undertaking of enormous magnitude.

When Navy Mobile Construction Battalion Ten landed with the Fourth Marine Regimental Landing Team at Chu Lai to construct an all-weather expeditionary airfield, it found the site covered with shifting wind-blown dunes of quartzite sand. The use of pneumatic-tired equipment was severely restricted, and the amount of earthwork required to level the site presented a serious problem, since speed was essential.

At Chu Lai, Navy Mobile Construction Battalion Ten was able to provide a continuously operational jet airfield while conducting extensive experimental work for the future use of AM–2 aluminum matting (the successor to World War II pierced steel planking) runway designs. The original operational strip, 3,500 feet long, was laid on a laterite base 10 inches thick. Confined to a small beachhead area, the Seabees and marines had little choice of material, and the available laterite proved to be of a very poor quality. Although it was originally planned to use plastic membrane seal between the laterite and the matting, the plastic material was not available in time for the first section of runway. This 3,500-foot section, equipped with arresting gear, was laid without a seal under it. It was started on 7 May 1965 and completed in twenty-one days. By 3 July the Seabees and marines had constructed an entire 8,000-foot runway, an 8,000x36-foot taxiway, and an operational parking apron of 28,400 square yards. This airfield, however, eventually experienced base failure, and the laterite was replaced with soil cement.

The second major aluminum mat airfield in Vietnam, constructed by RMK–BRJ, was at the Air Force base at Cam Ranh Bay. A runway 10,000 feet long by 102 feet wide was constructed on an all-sand subgrade. Because of the experience at Chu Lai, particular attention was paid to the base under the matting. Extensive soil stabilization work, beginning on 22 August 1965, included flooding the sand with sea water and rolling to stabilize it so that the sand could support earthmoving and compaction equipment. Following compaction and grading, the base was sealed with bituminous material. Laying of matting began late in September, and the runway was completed on 16 October. With completion of the runway, a parallel taxiway, high-speed turnoffs, and 60,000 square yards of operational apron, all in AM–2 plank, the scheduled operational date of 1 November was met.

Another AM-2 runway, identical in size to the one at Cam Ranh, was constructed at Phan Rang. It was started in September 1965 by the 62d Engineer Construction Battalion. Once again, the quality of the base was first improved. At this field a graded fill material was placed beneath the matting, and for the first time flexible plastic membrane was used as a seal. The first aircraft landed on the runway on 20 February 1966. The entire 10,000x102-foot runway was completed on 15 March, along with sufficient taxiways and aprons to provide an operational jet airfield. Later base failures, however, caused extensive reworking on the original airfield.

Believing that the Navy contractor would be unable to meet occupancy dates for some of their projects in Vietnam, the Air Force in February 1966 requested authority from the Secretary of Defense to make a separate contract with a U.S. firm for construction of an air base. Air Force officers detailed the scope of work but did not identify the site at meetings with potential contractors. The agreement they proposed to use was a "turnkey" contract whereby the contractor assumed responsibility for shipping and logistic requirements as well as for design and construction.

General Westmoreland and Admiral Sharp both opposed the introduction of another cost reimbursable construction contractor into Vietnam, arguing first that the air base was unnecessary and second that the proposed turnkey arrangement would bring one more construction organization into the country to compete for port facilities, storage, transportation, and other logistic support. The Secretary of the Navy supported General Westmoreland by pointing out to the Secretary of Defense that any scheme for increasing contract construction in Vietnam should take advantage of the existing capability of RMK-BRJ. On 12 March 1966 General Westmoreland reiterated his reasons for nonconcurrence with the Air Force proposal, and the following day Admiral Sharp endorsed General Westmoreland's position.

On 21 April, after being directed to reconsider the situation by the Joint Chiefs, General Westmoreland concluded that an additional airfield could be used. The preferred site was at Hue, but because this site was unavailable he recommended to Admiral Sharp that work start at Tuy Hoa.

On 27 April the Joint Chiefs of Staff consented to agree on Tuy Hoa, only if the Hue site was completely out of the question. They agreed to help surmount State Department objections to the Hue project but, in the interests of speed, urged that preliminary work be pushed at both locations. Responding to this message on 6 May, General Westmoreland mentioned Chu Lai as an acceptable alternative to Hue and concurred in proceeding with the Tuy Hoa site using the turnkey concept, as well as with a parallel runway at Chu Lai using the Navy's contractor.

On 7 May 1966 Admiral Sharp approved the Tuy Hoa proposal but imposed certain conditions. The Air Force's turnkey contractor would be responsible for building the complete Tuy Hoa complex —air base, port, and breakwaters—as well as for relocating roads and trackage. He would mobilize his own equipment, manpower, materials, and dredges, using only such local resources as were surplus to other service requirements. He would also be responsible for his own sea lift, unloading, beaching, and barging. In late May the Joint Chiefs of Staff gave the project their blessing, and on the 27th of that month the Deputy Secretary of Defense authorized the Air Force to negotiate a turnkey contract for the Tuy Hoa air base.

At Tuy Hoa, an 8-inch soil cement base was planned under the AM-2 aluminum mat. The airfield facilities included a 150x9,000-foot runway, a parallel taxiway 75 feet wide, and some 165,000 square yards of apron, with lighting, markers, and barriers. A control tower, operations buildings, and a communication facility were included. At first, a mobile tower and portable navigational aids were to be used. Fuel was handled through a 300,000-gallon "bladder system" until welded steel tanks were ready.

In all, five major jet air bases were constructed in Vietnam to supplement the three already in existence, and over 100 widely dispersed fields were built for intratheater transport aircraft. The major air bases afforded the necessary facilities for tactical aircraft and aircraft arriving from outside Vietnam, while the smaller fields allowed dispersal of logistics in support of forces operating in the field. The newly developed aluminum matting and older steel planking allowed construction at the most remote sites and permitted air delivery by heavier fixed-wing aircraft.

By mid-1966 the plan was to have every point in South Vietnam within twenty-five kilometers of an airfield. (*See Map 8.*) The few existing outlying airfields had been constructed mainly by the French. These strips were paved with a surface treatment from one-half to one inch thick and could not withstand the heavy volume of traffic required during tactical operations. In some of these operations up to 100 tons of supplies and 200 aircraft sorties were required daily.

The very nature of the war scattered small troop detachments to outlying locations. These detachments were supplied by air, primarily by CV-2 Caribou aircraft which were capable of landing on 1,000-foot hastily constructed airfields. Most of the early forward airfields were constructed with expedient surfacing materials such as

Two Caribous *debark troops on unimproved runway.*

laterite and crushed rock, which later proved to be inadequate. These surfaces had been used because a suitable matting was unavailable at the time of construction. M8A1 matting later was used extensively for forward airfields, although it required considerable maintenance when used by heavily loaded aircraft.

Forward airfield construction was rough and crude. Yet, experience indicated that the construction of each airfield should be preceded by as detailed a reconnaissance as time and circumstances would permit. In almost all instances the reconnaissance was made by helicopter. Landing permitted cone penetrometer soil-bearing tests and clearing and grading estimates. Time on the ground was usually limited to a few minutes because of possible enemy attack. With the ground survey completed, aircraft instruments were used to determine the runway azimuth and to estimate runway length.

Division operational plans and areas were often based on the availability of an airstrip that could be used by supporting fixed-wing aircraft and which was at or near the tactical operations area. Completion time was critical. Consequently, the reconnaissance was extremely important and accurate work estimates were essential.

Heliports varied in size from the brigade base camps of airmobile divisions to the isolated rearming and refueling facilities scattered about which have become common to the airmobile concept. While little preparation was required for a one-time landing zone in the forward areas, both the west and dry seasons in Vietnam posed significant problems in construction and maintenance of areas with a high density of helicopter traffic.

As with any piece of equipment, helicopter maintenance problems received command interest only after the abrasive effect of heavy dust was realized. Dust suppression was an obvious necessity for the safety of pilots during takeoffs and landings, and the damage dust caused to turbine blades was as effective as combat action, if not as dramatic, in downing aircraft. The use of matting or planking was effective in providing dust control, but unfortunately it was seldom feasible at hasty facilities constructed for helicopter operations. Periodic ground spraying with diesel fuel provided a relatively easy means of dust surpression for short periods of time, and usually some type of a trailer- or truck-mounted distributor could be manufactured for continued use by the using unit. Soil binders were effective for several weeks but were easily disturbed by vehicular traffic on the pad and could not withstand the monsoon season. The construction of a hardstand of asphaltic compounds or concrete offered a permanent solution and was considerably more economical in the long run than various types of portable matting.

The monsoon season also created many problems for heliports, which were often located in flat low-lying areas characterized by poor drainage. Considerable attention was required to ensure that all existing facilities would be usable, even after the very heavy monsoon rains. Both erosion and standing water had to be controlled or eliminated, and control of vehicular traffic through the heliport had to be regulated. Vehicles constituted a source of erosion and a safety hazard to approaching and departing aircraft, yet they were normally essential for aircraft maintenance and reprovisioning.

Much of the construction required to support aviation units was not included in early planning. Each aircraft in Vietnam eventually required a protective revetment. One of highest priorities in Vietnam during 1968 was the construction of protective structures for tactical aircraft. Known as the Hardened Shelter Program, the task of erecting these structures was assigned to Air Force Prime BEEF teams (base emergency engineering forces). The shelters eventually found most efficient in terms of unit cost (for fighter aircraft) were 72 feet long, 48 feet wide, and 24 feet high corrugated steel arch structures, which were covered with concrete for protection against rocket and mortar fire.

In the development of protective structures, particularly for helicopters, various designs were tested with the primary purpose of using materials indigenous to or readily obtainable in Southeast

MAP 8

Asia and of utilizing the manpower, skills, and equipment usually available to military field commanders. Vertical, sloping, and cantilever revetment walls were evaluated for their ability to protect against conventional weapons attacks. Construction procedures, requirements, and costs were studied, and basic weapons effects data pertinent to future protective structures were obtained.

Revetments did not provide complete protection for aircraft, but they did stop or deflect fragments. Only a cocoon-type enclosure, which in itself was able to resist both blast pressure and fragments, would completely protect an aircraft; but the cost of these structures, as well as the space occupied and the operational limitations imposed, made cocoons impractical as a solution for rotary-wing aircraft. Since some protection could be achieved with revetments alone, they were generally used. Protection against blast pressure, which might cause detonation of fuel and armament, had to be achieved by adequate spacing of aircraft. Considerable efforts were made to determine the most effective revetment. Earth-filled timber bins, cement-stabilized earth blocks, plain or cement-stabilized sandbags, sulphur and fiberglass coated cement blocks, soil-cement, and earth-filled fiberglass resin cylinders were the most suitable materials for revetment construction. Corrugated asbestos material with earth fill was effective against small arms fire; however, this brittle material was easily damaged by heavy weapons fire. Steel sheet piling without earth fill proved to be very ineffective in stopping small arms fire and fragments, but it had other drawbacks.

Seldom did economy or available construction materials permit much latitude in the selection of revetment types; the commander usually had to base his decision on erection time, equipment requirements, and the degree of protection desired. By the nature of their mission, aviation units have to relocate frequently, and each move required additional revetment construction. In Vietnam experience showed that approximately one-third of the units relocated annually. This mobility necessitated the use of prefabricated revetments which could easily be assembled, disassembled, and moved with the redeploying aviation units.

Use of M8A1 or other types of matting was considered justified to protect the enormously expensive aircraft, but investigation revealed that adequate protection was available with lower cost materials—particularly for rotary-wing aircraft. Corrugated sheet metal on 2×4 A-frames filled with earth proved to be effective, easy to construct, and relatively economical.

The use of precast concrete revetments was initiated in 1970. By this time precast yards were already manufacturing bridge decking, and the yards were easily converted to revetment fabrication.

Tests indicated these revetments were particularly effective and that they offered the advantage of long life and portability. From late 1970 on, the precast concrete revetment was adopted for exclusive use.

With construction in full swing, the size of bases continued to increase. The U.S. Navy complex at Da Nang in I Corps supported a powerful combined force. As of early 1968 more than two-thirds of the Navy's strength in Vietnam, or 22,000 men, were in I Corps, and the majority of them were in Da Nang. The Air Force had most of its 7,000 men in I Corps also stationed there. The port supplied the logistic support for the 1st and 3d Marine Divisions and several Marine support agencies. In all there were 81,000 marines being supported from the Da Nang complex in early 1968. As Army units moved north into I Corps in support of U.S., Korean, and Vietnamese forces, there would be seventy-three infantry battalions operating in these five provinces. The major facilities at Da Nang included:

1. The deepwater port.
2. The Naval Support Facility depot.
3. Jet airfields at Da Nang and Chu Lai.
4. A C-130 airfield at Hue.
5. Shallow LST ports at Chu Lai and Hue.

In late 1966 the Qui Nhon complex in II Corps supported combat operations of 15,100 combat troops (including 6,300 ROK) and 25,000 combat support troops (including 10,800 ROK) as well as service support elements numbering 22,100. Combat figures included some 550 Navy personnel engaged in coastal patrol and harbor defense. These men were part of the MARKET TIME operations. Cantonments were arranged so that all functional elements (combat, combat support and service) were grouped together. Major logistical and support facilities included:

1. Deepwater port with four berths at Qui Nhon.
2. Depot at Qui Nhon.
3. Jet airfields at Phu Cat and Tuy Hoa.
4. Five C-130 capable airfields at Kontum, Pleiku, Che Reo, Qui Nhon, and An Khe.
5. MARKET TIME facilities at Qui Nhon.

In late 1966 the Cam Ranh Bay complex in II Corps supported the operations of 8,000 combat troops (including 2,400 ROK) and 11,100 combat support troops (including 2,000 ROK), as well as 17,000 service support troops on a direct basis, and in addition provided general support backup for the entire theater. These

figures included 2,450 naval personnel supporting MARKET TIME, harbor defense, and the Naval Air Facility. The major logistical and support facilities included:
1. Deepwater port with ten berths at Cam Ranh.
2. Depot at Cam Ranh.
3. LST ports at Nha Trang, Phan Rang and Tuy Hoa.
4. Jet airfields at Cam Ranh Bay and Phan Rang.
5. Six other airstrips of which five were C–130 capable (Ninh Hoa: C–123 only).
6. MARKET TIME facilities.

In late 1966 the Saigon complex for III and IV Corps Tactical Zones supported 39,700 combat troops (1,400 allies) and 18,300 (5,200 allies) combat support troops, as well as 42,800 service support troops. Operations included MARKET TIME and GAME WARDEN. The major logistical and support facilities included:
1. Deepwater ports at Saigon (including Newport).
2. Depot at Saigon.
3. LST ports at Vung Tau and Can Tho.
4. Jet airfields at Tan Son Nhut and Bien Hoa.
5. Eight other airstrips of which five were C–130 capable.
6. MARKET TIME and GAME WARDEN facilities.

With the location of each major port of entry established on the concept of a series of logistical islands, each with easy access to the sea, the construction of more extensive base complexes proceeded apace. With no connecting roads and reliance on sea transportation for bulk supply, each island was a self-supporting unit capable of sustaining combat units in its immediate area of operations.

Until 1968 the I Corps Tactical Zone was under Navy and Marine Corps jurisdiction for the most part, with only a small Army contingent on hand. In the other three tactical zones in South Vietnam, the area support commands in Saigon, Qui Nhon, and Cam Ranh Bay operated under Army command, the Navy maintaining smaller facilities for the support of naval combat and patrol operations but obtaining items of common supply from Army stocks. After the spring of 1968 the Army moved in force into the I Corps Tactical Zone, basing its support operations at the already functioning base at Da Nang.

As the troop commitment to Vietnam increased, the numbers of individual supply depots of the logistical island type multiplied; each of the area commands became the hub of a network of smaller depots, and the demand for construction at their lesser "subarea" commands progressed accordingly. From a mail-order supply operation supporting some 25,000 American troops in 1965, the system expanded into a complicated and functioning, though sometimes less than efficient, machine supporting over a half million troops in three years' time.

CHAPTER VI

Facilities Construction

The vast construction effort designed to provide Vietnam with ports and airfields capable of accepting freight carriers did not encompass all that was necessary to provide for adequate handling of matériel once it did arrive. Mass movement of supplies and shortage of storage areas and of construction capability caused large quantities of supplies in early shipments to be stored in the open. This in turn caused rapid deterioration and losses. A more balanced effort of depot and port construction would have prevented some of the supply problems experienced later. However, the construction resources available had to be used where they were most urgently needed at the time. The tactical decision to bring in combat troops ahead of support units was necessitated by the enemy situation and political decisions which greatly complicated the problem of logistic and construction support.

The limited local facilities available for the buildup were not constructed to serve as warehouses, and their use precluded a well-organized supply effort. In August 1967, 25 percent of the required covered storage space was available, and another 43 percent was under construction. The lack of covered storage space was a prime contributing factor to deterioration of stocks. Space limitations and multiple storage locations were a major cause of lost stocks, poor inventory counts, and inefficient warehouse operations. In a climate like Vietnam's, high priority should have been given to early construction of covered storage space.

In April 1966, when the Qui Nhon Support Command was elevated to a depot command coequal with Cam Ranh, requirements were increased for storage facilities. Raymond, Morrison-Knudsen was then called upon to construct them; simultaneously, much of the work on depot facilities at Pleiku was turned over to RMK. The depot facilities requirements for Cam Ranh Bay were still not sufficient.

Perishable items in Vietnam were phased into the menu faster than storage and handling could be provided. Means of remedying this situation included leasing commercial facilities, using banks of hastily erected 1,600 cubic foot refrigerator boxes, and using offshore floating refrigerated storage. In September 1966 two cold storage warehouses were completed in Da Nang. In 1967 cold storage warehouses were completed in Cam Ranh Bay and Qui Nhon. In July 1969 the first section of the Long Binh cold storage warehouse was placed in operation with the rest becoming operational in October 1969. The construction of cold storage warehouses was definitely more economical than leasing facilities or using floating storage for extended periods of time, but cold storage facilities had to wait their turn among other priorities.

Since local ice production was limited, sixteen ice plants were brought into Vietnam in January 1966 and an additional twenty-four ice plants in July 1966. Because construction effort was lacking, erection of some of these plants was delayed, but many were erected by the facilities contractor, Pacific Architects and Engineers. Each ice plant was capable of a daily production of fifteen tons; yet, because local operating personnel were untrained, production was consistently below the plant's rated capacity.

To provide the wide range of dairy products in the quantity required in A rations, recombining milk plants were built in Vietnam. A Foremost Dairy plant began production in Saigon in December 1965. Under a contractual agreement with the Army, Meadowgold Dairies constructed a plant in Cam Ranh Bay, which began production on 15 November 1967, and a plant in Qui Nhon, which began production on 4 February 1968. After the cost was amortized, ownership was to be transferred to the U.S. government. By assuming the risk of operations, the Army obtained the Meadowgold product at a lower cost (including amortization costs) than the Foremost product. But in either case, the attempt at improving living conditions was appreciated.

In early 1966 considerable construction effort was directed into the upgrading of living facilities from field to intermediate standards. By pouring concrete tent slabs and constructing tropicalized buildings for mess halls, dispensaries, showers, and latrines, the transition was begun. In many cases, engineer troops prefabricated and erected buildings; in other cases, facilities were built by contract with Raymond, Morrison-Knudsen and Pacific Architects and Engineers, or by self-help with the technical assistance of engineer units.

By February 1966 cantonment construction was well under way. At Qui Nhon a 900-man cantonment for the logistical command and a 50-man cantonment for a signal relay site were in process. A division cantonment was under construction at An Khe. Cam Ranh's construction included a 6,400-man logistics camp and a 2,500-man engineer cantonment. At Phan Rang a 4,500-man cantonment was going up. Quonsets on pads for II Field Force headquarters were being constructed at Long Binh. Near Di An a 2,950-man cantonment for 1st Division units was in process. By mid-April 1966, construction had been expanded to include a 1,600-man cantonment at Dong Ba Thin, a brigade cantonment at Long Thanh, a 4,500-man cantonment at Lai Khe, and a drainage and roadnet at Cu Chi. By June 1966 in Qui Nhon, materials for cantonment construction were also supplied to a newly arrived Korean unit. Additional troop and contract construction at this time included a camp for a Korean headquarters unit at Nha Trang and a 4,500-man Australian cantonment at Vung Tau.

The decision to station U.S. ground troops in the delta south of Saigon led to the construction of a base camp at Dong Tam—a major undertaking because the site had to be elevated several feet. The dredging operation alone required several months. Construction began in mid-1966, and the first occupants moved in early in 1967. The first units arrived on LST's and other river craft in a carefully planned operation. Concurrent with the over-the-beach arrival of combat units, engineer units arrived by road and replaced an Eiffel bridge on the highway between Dong Tam and My Tho with a Bailey bridge. This opened up the road to Dong Tam, which was at this time the base camp for one brigade of the 9th Infantry Division. Another brigade was quartered on reconditioned barges provided by the U.S. Navy. These two brigades comprised the riverine assault group, which carried American forces into the delta.

By early 1967 approximately one quarter of the troops in Vietnam were in billets constructed by the Army Engineer Command, Vietnam. By about the same time 2,500 structures were built using self-help. Engineers provided equipment and supervision and constructed any facilities requiring special skills. The work began with the fabrication of major structural sections at engineer prefabrication sites. The engineer unit erected the first building while the self-help unit observed. After this demonstration, the using unit would designate work crews and begin construction. A construction engineer inspector was assigned to all projects to ensure proper workmanship and construction methods, while engineers installed drainage facilities, did excavation and grading, and poured more concrete pads. The self-help program evolved from an insatiable demand for engineer and construction resources. Self-help provided units with facilities sooner than would otherwise have been possible.

A study made by the U.S. Army, Vietnam, in 1966 recognized that cantonment construction involved more than clearing an area. Roads, billets, mess halls, latrines, showers, dispensaries, helicopter pads, water towers, chapels, and post offices would also have to be

QUARTERS *rise on concrete slabs at Long Binh.*

built sooner or later. This study defined a cantonment and determined the costs per man for each cantonment category. It also provided initial cost estimates for a typical infantry division cantonment constructed by troops at the following costs per man:

Field	Intermediate	Temporary
$240.00	$560.00	$940.00

Subsequently, on 20 October 1966, MACV Directive 415–1 establishing revised construction standards for cantonments in Vietnam was issued.

In 1967 General Westmoreland on a visit to Phan Rang expressed concern about the extent of new construction under way for units assigned to the 101st Airborne Division. He pointed out that much of the work was unnecessary because the 101st was almost constantly in the field and did not make full use of the buildings already erected. After his visit, General Westmoreland ordered all construction stopped at Phan Rang. Lieutenant General Bruce Palmer, Jr., then Deputy Commanding General, USARV, established a base development study group in August 1967 to study further the problem throughout the Army area. He asked the group to evaluate all base camp construction in light of current strengths and austere requirements. As a result of this review, numerous

FACILITIES CONSTRUCTION

reprograming actions were made to assure that only essential base construction continued.

In late September 1967 General Palmer approved the "hotel" concept recommended by the study group. The essence of this concept was that in any given base camp the Army would not try to accommodate every man stationed there, since a significant part of every maneuver unit would always be in the field. Capacity would be governed by the size of the population inhabiting a particular camp on a continuous basis. The hotel concept did present some problems in storage and maintenance facilities, however, since they were not initially constructed to accommodate all of the equipment and property left behind by units gone to the field.

The hospital program in the meantime consisted of a 1,000-bed convalescent hospital, which later expanded to 2,000 beds at Cam Ranh Bay, two 500-bed hospitals at Qui Nhon, one 500-bed hospital at Vung Tau, and a mobile surgical hospital at An Khe. In addition, various smaller facilities and field hospitals were being built throughout the country. Many of these hospitals were constructed by joint troop and contractor efforts. It was planned that most of the major troop cantonments or base complexes would have either a 60-bed surgical hospital or a 400-bed evacuation hospital. Field hospitals and convalescent centers were also constructed. (*See Map 9.*)

When the 45th Surgical Hospital arrived at Tay Ninh in October 1966, it was the first medical unit, self-contained, trans-

SPIDERLIKE DUCTS *provide air to MUST hospital complex from centralized air-conditioning units.*

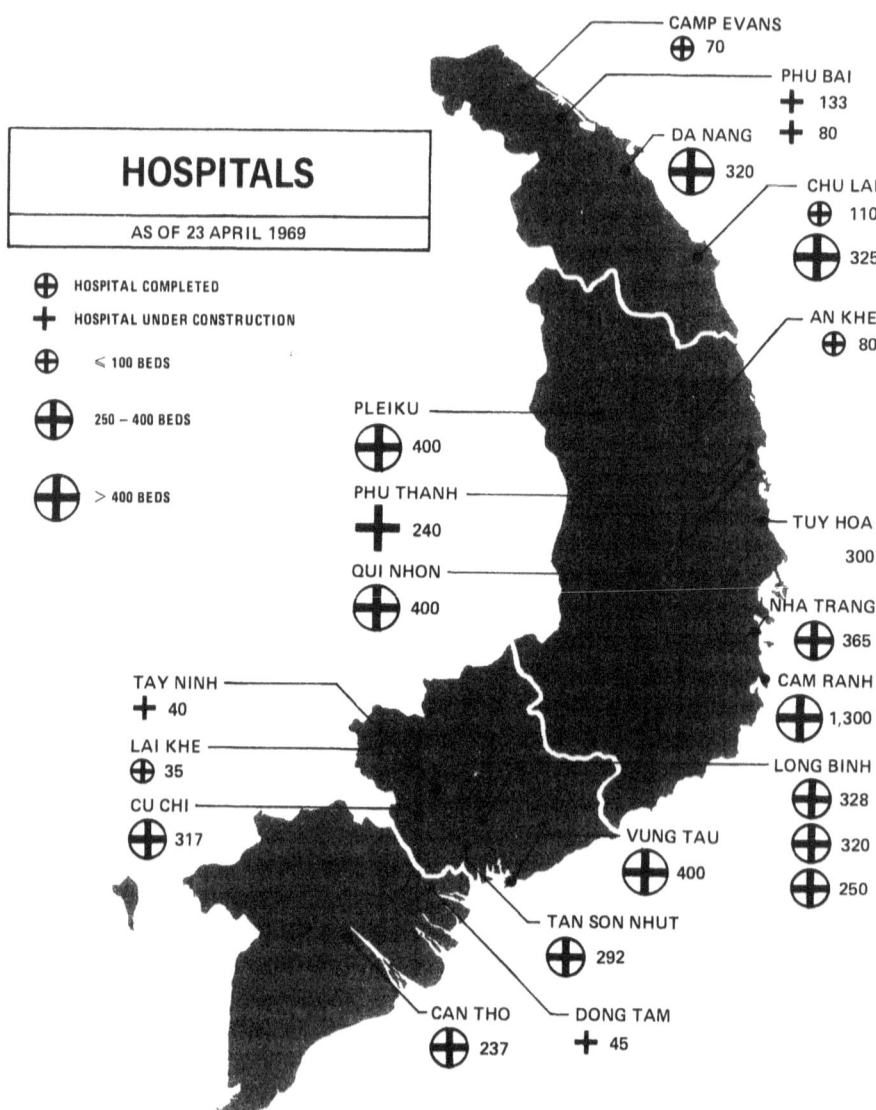

MAP 9

portable (MUST) hospital in Vietnam. This hospital was installed in a 500x1,000-foot area which contained all hospital facilities, billets for medical personnel, mess halls, and helipads. The hospital, developed by Garrett Air Research Company for the Army Medical Corps, was erected on a 200x300-foot laterite hardstand. The unit consisted of three separate packages, each weighing about 4,000 pounds, and was transportable by 2½-ton trucks. Enemy mortar fire showed that these facilities required additional protection; they were reinforced to withstand direct hits by 82-mm. mortar rounds.

Beginning in 1965 the administrative elements used existing facilities primarily in and around Saigon. However, as the buildup continued and forces spread throughout the country, more administrative facilities became a necessity—especially near logistical and major command centers. This construction was normally accomplished by the contractor or a contractor-troop combination. Administrative centers were built in Saigon, Tan Son Nhut, Long Binh, Cam Ranh, Qui Nhon, and Nha Trang.

Early in 1967 General Westmoreland began a campaign to reduce materially U.S. troop presence in major cities—especially Saigon. Under the direction of the MACV J-4, a program with the code name MOOSE (move out of Saigon expeditiously) was established. The program, however, was extremely difficult to implement. The first problem was to locate additional space outside of the city in an area where the same mission could be performed. Commanders were reluctant to leave the Saigon area and be very far away from the center of activity, that is, Military Assistance Command and Joint General Staff headquarters. Whenever a unit moved from leased quarters, there was always a tendency for other units, which were crowded, to expand into the vacated space.

Nevertheless by mid-1967, approximately half of the Army personnel was moved out of Saigon and relocated at the Long Binh complex. Personnel who remained were located primarily at Tan Son Nhut or were involved in activities which required close proximity to the air base or MACV headquarters. On 15 July 1967, USARV headquarters officially announced its move to Long Binh while construction crews still hurried to finish the facilities. Engineer troops graded and sodded the headquarters area to control erosion; established temporary water supply points; built three officers' mess halls, a VIP heliport, latrines and showers for enlisted personnel, and three trailer courts for general officers, VIP's, and senior colonels; erected flag poles; graded parking lots; and finished the access roads to the new USARV headquarters. Meanwhile, the contractor was completing the last headquarters building and working on the waterborne sewage system.

As headquarters and base camps grew, the entire Pacific Command communications system was expanded and upgraded. The environment and nature of operations gave rise to an extensive communications network within Vietnam. High-quality communications were required not only in Southeast Asia and by deployed combat forces in the western Pacific, but by other support elements scattered throughout the Pacific Command. An integrated communications system in support of operations in Vietnam was established, which extended from Hawaii to Korea in the north, Vietnam and Thailand in the south, and along the island chain from the Philippines to Japan.

In order to implement these systems, the construction of new semifixed facilities at various locations throughout Vietnam was necessary. This was accomplished both by troops and by the contractors. Installation of tools, test equipment, and work areas was performed by contract with Page Communications Engineers, Inc., whose services facilitated installation of fixed communications equipment during the buildup's initial stages and provided continuity of operations and technical expertise while the military were engaged elsewhere.

Without contractor support in the construction and installation of the fixed communications systems in Vietnam, effectiveness would have been considerably lessened. The military services, unfortunately, have relied on contractor support in the United States in recent years to such an extent that the services have failed to train personnel and equip sufficient units to perform these tasks for themselves. Other benefits were provided by the contractor effort in the construction, installation, operation, and maintenance of fixed communications. Contractor personnel remained in the country longer than the one-year tour served by military personnel, thus lending more experience and continuity to the job. The contractor also generally had access to other than military supply channels, and this facilitated his obtaining urgently needed repair parts and other supplies from any source directly.

For each major base constructed, and to a lesser extent for each of the smaller bases, the Army had to provide electrical power to run the unending variety of electrical machinery employed by a field army. There was a severe general shortage of commercial power throughout Vietnam. As units arrived in the country, they often had to get along with their own tactical generators. As cantonments were built and refrigeration plants, computer systems, communications sites, and similar facilities were added, standard Army generators simply could not meet the demand. So in 1966, 600 nontactical generators arrived from Japan, and another 722 were shipped from the United States. These generators ranged in size from 100 to 1,500 kilowatts. In March of the same year, a contract was awarded to the Vinnell Corporation to withdraw eleven T-2 tankers from the Maritime Reserve Fleet and convert them to floating electric power generating barges. Five of the converted ships were capable of generating 3,100 kilowatts, and six 4,300 kilowatts.

FACILITIES CONSTRUCTION

Five of the ships were eventually anchored at Cam Ranh Bay (15,500 kilowatts), and two each were located at Qui Nhon, Vung Tau, and Nha Trang (8,600 kilowatts at each location). In April 1966 the Vinnell Corporation began work on land-based electrical generation and distribution systems for Cam Ranh Bay, Qui Nhon, Nha Trang, Vung Tau, and Long Binh. This contract was modified in 1967 to provide service at twelve additional sites.

Despite these projects, demands for electrical energy continued to exceed supply as more and more sophisticated electrical equipment and machinery arrived in Vietnam, standards of living grew higher, and nice to have but largely unnecessary appliances—hot plates, toasters, air conditioners, coffee makers, and the like—appeared in post exchanges.

Air-conditioning equipment was also a critical item. Facilities requiring a controlled environment such as field hospitals and computer centers made large-scale installation of air conditioning necessary. There were widespread efforts to obtain air-conditioning equipment for quarters, open messes, and administrative areas. In an effect to reduce the diversion of air-conditioning equipment from essential purposes and also to reduce the maintenance load placed upon PA&E by widespread installation of air-conditioning equipment, USARV established a control system to ensure that air-conditioning equipment was not issued unless a control number

FLOATING POWER PLANTS. *Five tanker-generator ships providing power to Cam Ranh facilities.*

was assigned indicating that the equipment had been approved for a specific project.

Long-range planning for joint use of power systems had been further complicated by the fluctuation of troop deployments. Assets were constantly being reprogramed as planned unit base camps were changed in either size, location, or priority. In Nha Trang, for example, it proved impractical to service Air Force facilities from the planned T–2 tanker power plant, since the Air Force installation was based on a different primary system. At Cam Ranh the Army complex consisting of a convalescent center, replacement center, rest center, and other facilities was located a long distance from the T–2 electrical plant. It was also separated from the main Army installation to the south by a concrete runway. The Air Force was faced with the problem of serving its facilities on either side of the runway. In order to avoid constructing two Air Force power plants and a separate Army plant, an agreement was negotiated under which the Air Force would construct one power plant north of the runway and provide 5,000 kilowatts of power to the Army complex, while a like amount of power would be supplied to Air Force units south of the runway from the Army system.

A review of the T–2 power program in early 1967 showed slow progress. At Cam Ranh Bay five converted T–2 tankers were in position. Two were connected to the distribution system with a third to be tied in within three weeks. The primary distribution system was nearly completed. Power was being delivered to areas where the secondary system was installed. The remaining work consisted of completing the secondary distribution system, the 8,800-kilowatt land-based power plant, and the switching station. The completion date would be 1 May 1967. Total power was 33,800 kilowatts.

Two T–2 tankers for Qui Nhon were not yet positioned in early 1967. Dredging of the mooring site was in progress. The contractor was in the early phases of constructing pole lines. Completion was set for 1 July 1967. Total power would be 15,000 kilowatts. At Long Binh T–2 power ships had been scratched from the project and relocated. The Vinnell Corporation was mobilized and had started pole-line construction. Generator pads were being poured, and the first increment of power was scheduled for April 1967. Total power delivered would be 30,000 kilowatts with provisions for adding on 15,000 kilowatts. Two T–2 tankers for Nha Trang were in Vietnam but not positioned. Power output was to be 15,000 kilowatts. At this time one of the T–2 tankers was on hand for Vung Tau, and the last of the eleven ships was expected to depart the United States shortly. *(Map 10 and Table 3)*

FACILITIES CONSTRUCTION

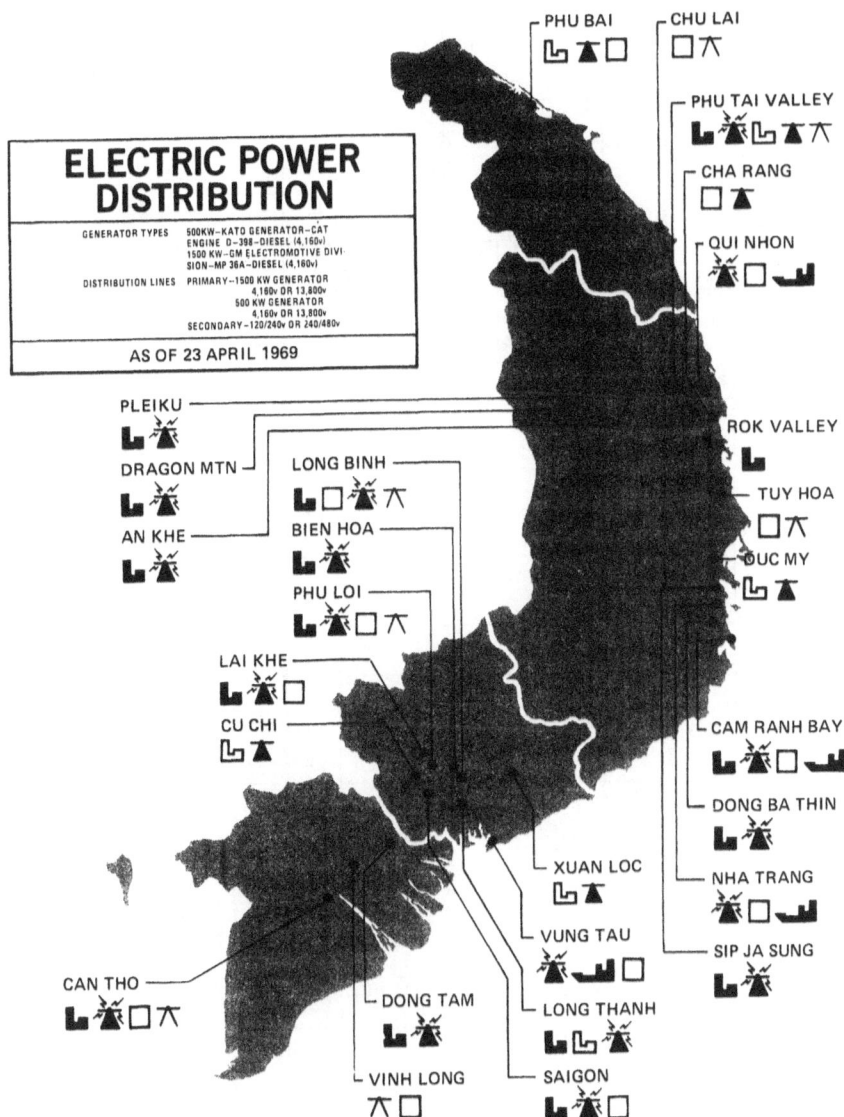

MAP 10

Real-estate problems were encountered at the various sites because of poor co-ordination. Vinnell had been doing the design work for distribution systems in the United States and had not made field checks on the positioning of switching gear, transformer stations, power lines, or other factors which would affect the area that the power grid would occupy. The contracting officer's representa-

TABLE 3—ELECTRIC POWER DISTRIBUTION

LOCATION	IN PLACE									UNDER CONSTRUCTION							PROPOSED				
	Generators, KW			Power Barges, KW			Total KW	Distribution, LF		Completion Date	Generators, KW			Total KW	Distribution, LF		Estimated Date of Completion	Generators, KW			Total	Distribution, LF		Estimated Date of Completion
	500	1500		5000	7500			Primary	Secondary		500	1500			Primary	Secondary		500	1500			Primary	Secondary	
PHU BAI											6			3,000	1,200	1,500	APR 69	3			1,500	55,000	52,000	(5) DEC 69
CHU LAI																		6			3,000			
CHA RANG															26,000	19,030	AUG 69	5			2,500			SEP 69
PLEIKU-LOG DEPOT	4						2,000	42,000	19,000	JAN 69														
PLEIKU-DRAGON MT		6					9,000	74,460	68,000	JAN 69														
AN KHE		6					9,000	114,650	74,500	NOV 68														
PHU TAI VALLEY "F"		3					4,500	39,045	19,180	JAN 69														
PHU TAI VALLEY "R"																								(1)
PHU TAI VALLEY "G"																					10,000	6,000		
QUI NHON				2			15,000	122,000	31,700	FEB 68	8			4,000	25,000	20,000	JUL 69							
ROK VALLEY		4					6,000	63,200	67,840	JAN 69									5/1		9,000	17,000	40,000	(4)/(5)
TUY HOA																			3		4,500			SEP 69
DUC MY-NINH HOA	6						3,000	36,600	28,800	NOV 68	3			1,500	53,000	30,000	JUN 69	69						
SP/ASUNG-ROK NHA TRANG				2			15,000	86,200	25,400	FEB 68								12/3		7,500	16,000		(4)/(5)
NHA TRANG																								
DONG BA THIN	4						2,000	17,000	11,000	DEC 68														(4)
CAM RANH BAY	4			5			33,800	294,700	104,400	MAR 68								4	9	13,500	16,000	25,000		(3)
LAI KHE							2,000	100,000	95,040	NOV 68										2,000				
PHU LOI	3						1,500	14,000	3,000	NOV 68														
CU CHI		3					4,500	47,470	37,700	DEC 68	12			6,000	62,000	100,000	JUN 69	3		1,500				JUL 69
BIEN HOA																								
LONG BINH		21					31,500	406,000	171,000	DEC 68					25,000	16,000			6/3	13,500				(4)/(5)
XUAN LOC-BLACK HORSE	3						1,500			JUL 67	6			3,000	42,000	50,000	SEP 69	2		1,000				(5)
SAIGON-3rd Fld Hosp.																								
SAIGON-NEW PORT	3						1,500	50,000	59,000	NOV 67														
LONG THANH	3						4,500	94,000	90,000	DEC 68		3		4,500			APR 69	3		1,500				(5)
DONG TAM	12						6,000	43,000	37,000	MAR 69				2,000										
VUNG TAU																		12		6,000	18,000	18,000	(4)	
VINH LONG		4			2		15,000	92,000	86,700	DEC 67								3/1		2,000			SEP 69/(3)	
CAN THO							2,000	44,000	22,000	DEC 68								4		2,000	44,000	22,000	JAN 70	
TOTAL	43	46		5	6						35	3						57/4	23/4					

(1) AWAITING USARV DECISION ON CANCELLATION; (2) AWAITING MACV DECISION; (3) AWAITING MACV APPROVAL; (4) AWAITING OSD APPROVAL; (5) FUTURE REQUIREMENT
* INCLUDING 8 EA. 1,100 KW LAND BASED GENERATORS'

tive in Vietnam subsequently initiated the appropriate real-estate acquisition procedures and managed to co-ordinate the space available with the size of the power system.

At division base camps, it was extremely difficult to provide enough power with small generators. Practically all of the large bases eventually had high-voltage central power systems operated by one of the contractors. This proved very efficient and satisfactory in the long run; however, the system would be extremely difficult to operate and maintain if untrained military units had to be used.

Since water supply has a very direct effect on the health and the welfare of troops, as various fixed Army installations in Vietnam were being created, expanded, and improved, so was the water supply. When U.S. forces began arriving in Vietnam, it was necessary to rely on water sources that were immediately available; these included lakes, rivers, streams, shallow wells, and occasionally municipal systems. These surface water sources were all subject to contamination and were of a generally poor quality, and the water obtained required extensive treatment. Existing well locations usually required hauling water over congested routes for long distances, and since water supply points were usually located outside cantonment areas the enemy could interdict them and deny their use.

Water was treated with tactical erdlators, which provided coagulation, sedimentation, filtration, and chlorination. Although the annual rainfall is heavy in Vietnam, and there are abundant surface water sources, the amount of water available for troop consumption was limited by treatment capability. To overcome these disadvantages, a massive deep-well drilling program was initiated. It was anticipated that these wells, producing water from deep underground sources, would provide water of better quality so that no treatment other than chlorination would be required.

The deep-well program did improve water quality, and water production was increased. The aim was fifty gallons per man per day. Supply sources were relatively secure, since the new wells were located within cantonment areas. The relocation of wells and water points and the improved distribution systems released erdlators and purification units for use by tactical units in those areas where surface sources were still in use.

The well-drilling program made use of both military and civilian contractor drilling teams. The first phase of the program in early 1967 envisioned the drilling of 180 wells throughout Vietnam with a cost of approximately $5.4 million. At that time there were seventeen civilian, five Army, and four Navy well-drilling rigs and teams working in the country. In addition to providing water, this project furnished important hydrological information on subsurface conditions throughout the country. From this information, the second phase of the program was formulated, and additional wells were dug. A production goal of fifty gallons per man per day for intermediate and field cantonments and a hundred gallons per man per day for temporary cantonments was achieved in most locations.

Many problems were encountered in implementing the well-drilling program. Contractors had difficulties in obtaining permission for their employees to enter Vietnam and trouble assembling supplies. The Army teams lacked experience and faced a continual shortage of well supplies such as casing and screen. However, through practice and various expedient methods the problems of the Army were finally overcome.

Contract well-drilling was phased out on 15 April 1967. Contractors had completed approximately 160 of the 300 wells programed. The rest of the program was carried on with four Seabee-operated drill rigs and seven Army drill rigs. Together they drilled 68 additional wells, bringing the number of wells to 248. This completed about 75 percent of the well-drilling program. These Seabees left for the United States on 30 September 1967, and the remainder of the program was completed by Army detachments.

Central waterborne sewage systems were originally provided at very few locations. The burn-out latrine, locally manufactured from a 55-gallon drum cut in half and partially filled with diesel fuel, was used at sites not located within or near major cities. Burn-out latrines were inexpensive to construct and operate and met field standards of sanitation. But morale was adversely affected by this primitive outdoor plumbing with its inevitable odors and by the dense, foul, black smoke generated during burning. Troops were particularly disgruntled when they had to burn out latrines in areas restricted to Vietnamese workers. Morale also suffered considerably in areas such as Cam Ranh Bay where on one side of the bay the Army had burn-out latrines, and on the other side the Navy and Air Force had a central system.

In July 1967 a sewage lagoon for primary and secondary treatment of sewage for a population of 14,000 was constructed at Long Binh. Sewage lagoons, when properly operated, performed very well. The decomposition of sewage in lagoons eliminated both objectional odors and appearance.

Due to heavy rainfall and the soil encountered in Vietnam, normally used treatment facilities were not adequate. The possible exception to this was the trickling filter. Leaching fields and septic tanks did not always work properly, basically due to the general imperviousness of the soil. Oxidation ponds were not always prac-

LARC V, *amphibious cargo carrier.*

tical because the excessive land required was not always available due to heavy rainfall. These problems were further compounded by the high water table, which in most areas of Vietnam is within twelve to eighteen inches of the surface during the monsoon season.

Sanitary fill areas were established for all areas as land could be made available. Equipment for the operation of the fills was borrowed from somewhere else. Sewage disposal is still provided in most places away from heavily populated areas by burn-out latrines or septic tanks. Local-hire personnel handle latrines, while facilities contractor personnel pump septice tanks and operate the few waterborne sewage distribution systems.

During early stages of the buildup, U.S. military forces experienced other supply distribution problems. Ammunition supply was particularly critical because of the limited adequate storage facilities and great dispersion of forces. In March 1965 the only ammunition supply point in Vietnam was at Tan Son Nhut. By the end of the year eight air supply points had been constructed to receive emergency loads of ammunition in operations areas. Ships were waiting to unload, and there was an urgent requirement for the expansion of facilities. Due to their strategic locations, heavy traffic moved into the ports of Saigon, Qui Nhon, Da Nang, and Cam Ranh Bay. All deep-draft vessels entering these ports had to be discharged offshore, and the ammunition was brought ashore by lighters.

The situation became critical in December 1965, and steps were taken to relieve a 48,000-ton backlog, which was distributed at the ports of Saigon, Qui Nhon, Da Nang, and Cam Ranh Bay. Construction of a deepwater ammunition pier at Cam Ranh Bay started late in 1965, and improvement and expansion of ammunition offloading points at other ports eased the crisis somewhat, but even as late as 1969 facilities were still not totally adequate. Procurement of unnecessary real estate for dispersed storage of the quantities of ammunition shipped to Vietnam took time. Waivers were necessary to permit the continued on-the-ground storage of ammunition, since it was not possible to meet all safety criteria. Construction of adequate new ammunition storage facilities was subject to military construction procedures, priority allocations, and required lead times. The magnitude of the storage problem can be illustrated by citing stockage objectives established by the services during the peak of U.S. force buildup. These levels required in the country were 295,000 tons for the Army, 59,000 tons for the Air Force, and 56,000 tons for the Marine Corps. The total of 410,000 tons included neither Navy requirements nor provision for the large quantities of suspended and unserviceable ammunition requiring storage pending retrograde. Even then stockage objectives were often exceeded.

BARC, *the heaviest of the amphibious lighters.*

FACILITIES CONSTRUCTION

Because of the difficulty in obtaining adequate real estate, a modular concept of storage, which had been developed by the Air Force, was approved by General Westmoreland for use in the combat zone. In application, a module was comprised of a maximum of five cells, each separated by barricades. Each cell contained 100 tons of explosives. This allowed the storage of up to 500 tons of explosives in a single contiguous module. Separate revetments were limited to 125 tons each. This resulted in decreased land requirements and reduced the distance requirement between explosive storage areas and other facilities.

Although the modular ammunition storage system provided a savings in space, it concentrated large quantities of ammunition in small areas and made for a greater hazard. The loss of several ammunition supply points due to fire and enemy action justified the need to continue attempts to find suitable methods for improving ammunition storage. The consequences of not taking action were well illustrated in the loss of the ammunition supply point at Da Nang on 27 April 1969 in which approximately 39,170 tons of ammunition valued at $96 million were lost in one attack.

Construction in Vietnam was only partly a process of converting bulk raw materials into facilities. The American construction industry conceived pre-engineering and prefabrication as a means of minimizing design requirements and increasing on-site productivity. Although building codes and labor agreements have slowed the adoption of prefab techniques in the American civilian sector, the services were under no constraints in the theater of operations. From a military viewpoint, a prefabricated package can be deployed at least as rapidly as bulk construction materials; it can be erected faster with fewer men; and its relocatability can reduce additional material requirements in redeployments. The shortage of engineer construction units in a future Vietnam-size contingency indicates that greater use must be made of this type structure.

In early 1966 a requirement for 12,000 pre-engineered buildings was determined for Vietnam. Specifications for some prefab structures were outdated and the buildings could not be provided expeditiously. Efforts were initiated to develop specifications and procure needed standardized pre-engineered buildings. By late 1966 both the Army and the Air Force were using the BUSH (Buy U.S. Here) Program and purchasing buildings for the Far East. The buildings eventually procured were of many different makes and types. These pre-engineered and prefabricated commercial-type facilities were used extensively in Vietnam for shops and warehouses in logistics and air base complexes. They were also used to meet administrative requirements in some of the large complexes,

A COMPLETE SELECTION *of wood, aluminum, and steel buildings under construction.*

such as the Military Assistance Command headquarters and the Long Binh headquarters of the U.S. Army, Vietnam. In some smaller complexes such as the Da Nang Supply Depot where real estate and time limitations dictated rapid erection of multistory structures, they also found users.

One type of prefabricated building used widely in the Long Binh area was the advanced design aluminum military shelter, an Australian development, popularly known as ADAMS huts, which were of all-aluminum construction and featured louvered sections in walls and windows for maximum ventilation. While ADAMS huts were easily erected on concrete slabs, they required the drilling of many holes on site to fasten the components together.

Use of modular buildings was more advantageous in many respects than construction on site of temporary structures. The main objection was the procurement cost which was substantially higher than a wooden structure built on the same site. However, the savings realized by purchasing relocatable structures and from cost reduction in erection time tended to offset high initial costs.

CHAPTER VII

Facilities Engineering

Facilities engineering, as distinct from new construction, refers to the series of operations carried out after basic structures are complete. It involves the services necessary to keep any large physical plant functioning efficiently: maintenance and repair of buildings, surfaced areas and grounds, service to refrigeration and air conditioning, minor ancillary construction, fire prevention, removal of trash and sewage, rodent and insect control, water purification, custodial services, management of property, engineer planning, supply of maintenance materials, and maintenance of equipment used in the upkeep of a base.

For these operations the Army relied heavily on civilian contractors working under an arrangement in which the contractor provided labor, organization, and management, while the Army provided tools, repair parts, supply, mess facilities, and quarters for the work force.

A number of factors influenced how facilities engineering support would be provided. Contingency planning for operations in Vietnam had not, in any of the joint service plans, developed a requirement for facilities engineering forces. While operations in Vietnam were substantially different from those assumed in developing contingency plans, the fact remained that plans were not developed to support facilities once erected during previous sessions of contingency planning. The inability to produce the manpower for a military facilities engineer force severely limited other military engineer capabilities from the outset. Most of the engineer utilities detachments intended for facilities engineering were in Reserve status, and the decision not to mobilize the Reserve meant that these forces would be unavailable. The strict limitations on personnel strength in Vietnam and the desire to keep the ratio of support troops as low as possible forced consideration of a predominantly civilian work force. However, low ceilings were imposed on direct hiring, a complex and slow procedure; this left a civilian contract force as the only feasible alternative. Consequently, with the buildup the Army called upon Pacific Architects and Engineers to expand its organization as the pace of facilities construction increased. The contractor's response was commendable, although not without problems. His strength grew from 274 men located at six adviser sites in 1963 to a peak strength of over 24,000 in 1968 at more than 120 locations.

The piecemeal nature of the buildup made it almost impossible to predict future requirements or even the eventual location of incoming troop units. The system which evolved was to tailor the contractor's organization to meet the needs of each installation as it was established and expanded. The PA&E work force was made up of a combination of U.S. civilians, Vietnamese, and other nationalities. The force mix was about 5 percent American, 15 percent other country, and 80 percent Vietnamese. The contract with PA&E grew to approximately $100 million per year, not including government-furnished supplies amounting to approximately $20 million.

While the Army relied heavily on Pacific Architects and Engineers, it knew that the contractor could not do all the work. His civilian workmen could not enter certain areas of the combat zone and would go off the job when curfews and strikes were ordered. There were, however, approximately 1,450 engineer troops mobilized and deployed in Vietnam as utilities detachments and firefighting and water purification teams. (*See Chart 5.*) Military power plant operation and water supply companies ranged in size from four to forty men. While some of these units operated at the same locations as the contractor's forces, they were stationed primarily in outlying areas where for security reasons civilians were barred.

In addition to the PA&E work force and the engineer utility detachments, there were a number of smaller contracts let for specific kinds of facilities engineering support. But, except for contracts with the Navy and Philco-Ford in I Corps and with Vinnell for electric power generation, these contracts will not be discussed individually.

In sharp contrast to the Army, the Air Force facilities engineering forces were predominantly military. During peacetime, the Air Force had maintained a significant number of military personnel as facility maintenance engineers in its stateside installations. This gave the Air Force a good base upon which to draw when the conflict in Vietnam developed. A base civil engineer force is an integral part of an Air Force wing, and when wings were deployed to Vietnam, their base maintenance forces went with them. These forces were augmented by Red Horse squadrons (heavy maintenance and repair units numbering about 400 men) and Prime BEEF teams (small detachments sent for six-month tours to augment the base civil engineer forces for specific projects). The Air Force made considerable use of contracts, but these were usually for special tasks, such as power generation and refuse collection.

The Navy also experienced a shortage of trained military personnel, although it was somewhat better off than the Army in this regard. In I Corps, Seebees were assigned to the Public Works Department, Naval Support Activity, at Da Nang. The Seabees managed the work force augmented by hired foreign nationals and by local nationals provided under a service contract with Philco-Ford. The work force was made up of about one-third Seabees, one-third foreign nationals, and one-third Vietnamese. In contrast to the Army's contract with Pacific Architects and Engineers, the Philco-Ford contract served primarily to provide skilled local labor. Except at a few industrial facilities, the contractor was not responsible for over-all management. In addition to the forces assigned to the Public Works Department in Da Nang, the Navy activated two construction battalion maintenance units and sent them to Vietnam.

As previously noted, Pacific Architects and Engineers had to organize and staff its forces along the lines of standard Army organizations. To control this force, PA&E established a Contract Management Office in Saigon and three district offices at Saigon, Qui Nhon, and Cam Rahn Bay from which PA&E forces and operations at each Army installation were controlled. A highly effective communications net was operated independently of the unreliable Vietnamese telephone system and of the military communications system, which was needed for high-priority operational traffic.

SEABEES *responsible for bridge construction in I Corps.*

Administration of contracts and the technical direction and control of the contractor's activities were, until mid-1968, the responsibility of the 1st Logistical Command. Within the 1st Logistical Command, responsibility for contract management was vested in the U.S. Army Procurement Agency, Vietnam (USAPAV). The rapid growth of contract work between 1965 and 1967 made it evident that better control than the procurement agency and the 1st Logistical Command engineering staffs could provide was needed. Therefore, the Contract Operations Branch, located at PA&E's Contract Management Office in Saigon, was established as a part of the Office of the Engineer, 1st Logistical Command. In addition, the staff engineers of the Saigon, Qui Nhon, and Cam Ranh Bay Support Commands, subordinate commands of the 1st Logistical Command, and the staff engineers of the installations within the support command areas were delegated appropriate contracting officer's representative authority. The Contract Operations Branch consisted of an operations branch, a technical inspection branch, and a performance and analysis branch. It had the mission of directing the contractor's activities and analyzing contract operations and expenditures. This new organization facilitated the identification and resolution of many problems which resulted in increased efficiency and responsiveness in the contractor's work.

Increasing construction, real estate, and facilities engineering costs resulted in a decision to integrate all Army engineer activities in the U.S. Army Engineer Construction Agency, Vietnam (USAECAV), in 1968. In July 1968, USAECAV also assumed the facilities engineering responsibilities formerly assigned to the 1st Logistical Command except for a direct-hire force supporting the Saigon area under the direction of the U.S. Army Headquarters Area Command. This activity was also later transferred to USAECAV in 1969.

Under the Construction Agency organization, district engineer offices were established at Saigon, Cam Ranh Bay, and Qui Nhon. The district engineers, in turn, supervised the installation engineers. This provided a vertical command channel from USAECAV through the district engineers to the installation engineers independent of other command relationships. This vertical channel, together with a substantial increase in the number of military personnel directly concerned with supervision of the contractor's operations (212 under the Construction Agency as compared to 73 under the 1st Logistical Command), substantially improved operations management.

Under the new setup, 1st Logistical Command's procurement agency retained contracting officer authority, and the contracting officers, who exercised technical supervision over the contractor, reported to two separate headquarters. To overcome the inherent disadvantages in this arrangement, it was proposed to provide the Commanding General, USAECAV, with contracting officer authority for the facilities engineering contract. This, however, was disapproved by the Department of the Army in order to avoid fragmenting procurement authority in Vietnam. While this decision did not result in the optimum organizational relationships from the viewpoint of managing the facilities engineering effort, relations between the procurement agency and the construction agency under a memorandum of understanding were excellent. Through mutual effort, the difficulties inherent in the organizational relationship were minimized.

The form of the contract with PA&E underwent several changes. Originally negotiated as a cost plus a fixed fee in 1963, the contract remained in effect until 1970. To increase the contractor's incentive in performance of the contract, the Procurement Agency assisted by the Construction Agency negotiated a cost-plus-award-fee contract in 1969. Under this contract the company was evaluated on its performance, and the fee depended upon this evaluation. The new agreement appears to have resulted in increased effectiveness and efficiency.

An effort was made to introduce competition by splitting off the Qui Nhon area in 1968 and advertising for new bids. Because PA&E was already working in Vietnam and was familiar with facilities engineering operations there, the firm had a distinct advantage over any competitors. Consequently, the new contract also went to Pacific Architects and Engineers. The attempt to introduce competition not only proved unsuccessful, but the new contract meant PA&E would operate under two distinct contracts. Any thoughts of a second try at competition were quietly laid aside, and the following year the Army returned to a single contract.

In 1967 PA&E's activities were extended into I Corps following deployment of substantial numbers of Army units into the area, which had been primarily a Marine Corps and Navy zone of operations. Although the Navy was providing logistical support for I Corps, it was not in a position to support all Army installations.

In 1970, following major shifts in U.S. operations, logistical responsibility for I Corps was transferred from the Navy to the Army. Consideration was given to extending the PA&E contract to cover all of the area, but the decision was made to negotiate a contract with Philco-Ford to continue in the areas where they had been working under contract to the Navy. This arrangement facilitated continuity of operations but had the disadvantage of resulting in two different contracts and contractors to supervise.

Experience in Vietnam highlighted many administrative, regulatory, and other constraints, which indicated areas where improvement was required. Vietnam was the first conflict in which peacetime Army budget regulations had been stringently applied in a combat zone. Many of the peacetime regulations applicable to facilities engineering were necessarily prohibitive in nature and cumbersome in application. Designed to minimize the diversion of utilities engineering resources and to avoid certain statutory violations, the application of these regulations in a combat zone greatly inhibited the effectiveness of facilities engineering support by both the contractor and the utilities detachments. Further examination of these regulations as well as the Department of Defense directives and the laws on which they were based is required to achieve greater flexibility and responsiveness under future combat conditions.

The contractor, PA&E, frequently drew criticism for overstaffing. Much of his staffing requirements, however, resulted directly from the requirement that he organize, staff, and manage his efforts strictly in accordance with Army regulations. (*Chart 6*) This resulted in much of the contractor's effort going into work management and production control. While the principles of work management are an inherent part of effective operations under any conditions, the amount of effort expended in the preparation of detailed schedules and work plans was of questionable value under the turbulent conditions which prevailed. There was a distinct advantage in having the contractor follow Army regulations in organizing and managing his force in that this facilitated the control and monitoring by the contract officers, but here too consideration should be given to adopting simplified procedures for combat conditions.

A major problem that persisted throughout the conflict, largely because of the rapid turnover of military personnel, was the general lack of facilities engineering experience. The one-year tour of duty was necessary from a morale standpoint, but it had an adverse effect on the operations of the engineer detachments and on contractor supervision. Most officers assigned to facilities engineering duty in Vietnam lacked former experience, and it normally took much of their one-year tour to become knowledgeable in facilities engineering regulations and requirements. The Vietnam experience has highlighted the need for a broader base of both officers and enlisted men with facilities engineering training and experience.

Perhaps the greatest difficulty in the contractor's operations stemmed from the problems he had in obtaining the necessary government-furnished supplies and equipment—problems which were not resolved until late in the conflict.

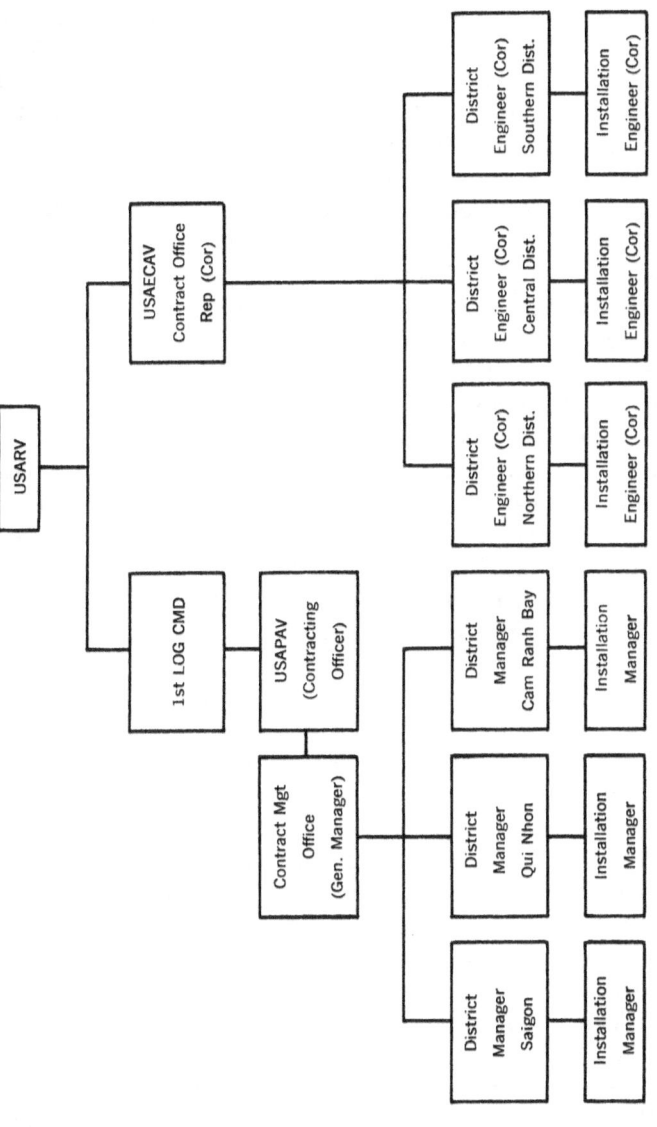

CHART 6—FACILITIES MAINTENANCE ORGANIZATION

Despite these difficulties, the facilities engineering support of combat forces in Vietnam was an undertaking successfully carried out on a scale never before seen in a combat zone. The rest of this chapter will discuss a few of the special problem areas.

While primarily contracted for facility operation, maintenance, and repair, PA&E was used extensively to accomplish construction of minor facilities during the major period of the troop buildup from mid-1965 to mid-1968. Before the buildup, the small PA&E force was primarily engaged in maintenance and repair of leased facilities. As more and more troop units arrived in Vietnam, the most urgent requirements were to construct defenses followed by troop and support facilities. Urgent requirements existed for cantonments, airfields, depots, repair shops, and the utilities systems needed to service them. Because of its construction capability, Pacific Architects and Engineers was called upon to provide help in small operations and maintenance funded (under $25,000) projects. Paradoxically, although much of its effort went into construction, the terms of the PA&E contract did not permit the contractor's employment on new construction funded work. This meant that he could not construct many of the facilities needed for his own use, which would have increased his over-all effectiveness. By the end of 1967 the increased capabilities of the construction contractors and construction troops made it possible for Pacific Architects and Engineers to concentrate on facilities engineering. The sharply increased demand for facilities engineering made redirection of PA&E effort imperative as more new facilities went into use and more troops arrived in the theater. While during 1965 and 1966 the contractor expended as much as 80 percent of his effort on new construction, this figure dropped to 25 percent by the middle of 1968 and to below 15 percent in subsequent years.

The varying standards of construction and the absence of a standard for maintenance and repair proved troublesome throughout the conflict. Although the Military Assistance Command in Vietnam published over-all standards, wide variations existed. Standards ranged from tent frames and Southeast Asia huts to elaborate air-conditioned, pre-engineered facilities with high-voltage electric distribution systems and modern water and sewage systems. The extent of facilities engineering support received by individual installations depended on what local commanders needed and on what facilities they succeeded in getting built. Until very late in the conflict, there were no countrywide standards for planning facilities engineering support. As a result, resources were often not equitably distributed.

Fire protection was certainly adequate at Army installations

VIETNAMESE FIREFIGHTER *ignores risk in fighting petroleum fire at Long Binh.*

throughout Vietnam. Fire companies were manned primarily by PA&E, although there were some military firefighting detachments. On a visit in 1969, representatives of the Office of the Chief of Engineers pointed out that there were far too many fire companies and fire trucks in the theater. Further analysis by the Army Engineer Construction Agency led to a substantial reduction in fire companies and the cancellation of all outstanding requisitions for fire trucks. Although fire protection was possibly overstressed, fire prevention was given inadequate attention. While temporary structures appropriate to a combat zone were constructed with combustible materials like plywood and low-density fiberboard, fire hazards could have been appreciably reduced by proper building-site spacing. Still, the use of combustible interior partitions and other interior finishes and nonexpert installation, extension, and modification of electrical systems created serious fire hazards. The lesson is evident—more emphasis must be given to fire prevention.

Control of insects, rodents, and other pests was a particularly challenging problem. Vietnam lacks all but the most basic health and sanitation safeguards; malaria and the plague are endemic. Vigorous efforts by facilities engineering entomology teams and the rigid enforcement of health and sanitation rules turned military bases into "islands of health in a sea of disease and pestilence." The return of retrograde cargo from Vietnam raised the danger of Asiatic insects and rodents being brought back. Careful and thorough cleaning of this cargo and treatment with rat poison and insecticide dust—as much as 112 tons per month—effectively eliminated this danger. Losses of foodstuffs in storage from insect infestation amounted to millions of dollars annually. During 1970, new control techniques for treatment of stored foodstuffs in CONUS before shipment and in Vietnam after receipt were adopted. Fumigation of railway cars in transit from the mills began in September 1970. Experience in the United States to date indicates that these procedures will reduce losses of stored foods by as much as 98 percent.

Chief among the lessons learned from Vietnam was that the requirements for facilities engineering support in future conflicts must be anticipated during contingency planning, inasmuch as these requirements represent a substantial portion of the resources required to support such an operation—the total force dedicated to facilities engineering (over 25,000) approached the combined strength of the two engineer brigades deployed to Vietnam (about 30,000). The feasibility and, under similar circumstances, the desirability of providing the major portion of this force by contract was demonstrated in Vietnam. Our experience also clearly demonstrated the need for the Army to maintain, in its active force structure, an adequate number of military personnel trained in facilities engineering to provide management and supervision of contractor and direct-hire civilian maintenance forces and to man sufficient numbers of military facilities engineering detachments to ensure continuity of essential operations in emergency situations.

CHAPTER VIII

The Road Programs

The extensive highway system in the Republic of Vietnam was constructed mainly during the past five decades. Before 1954, approximately 20,000 kilometers of roads existed, of which about 6,000 kilometers were national or interprovincial and 14,000 kilometers were rural or secondary roads. By the time of the cease-fire in 1954, most of the country's highway network had been destroyed, and long segments of the highway system had become impassable to motorized traffic. The highways that remained were generally inadequate for military usage because of either faulty design or poor surfacing. Most bridges were destroyed. The national highway system, particularly National Route 1, sustained the most damage. Six hundred and fifty kilometers of Route 1 from Phan Thiet to Hue were largely impassable. To reopen the road approximately 240 bridges with a total length of 11,295 meters had to be reconstructed, endless culverts installed, and thousands of cubic meters of fill had to be replaced where erosion had taken its toll.

In the government of Vietnam, the Director General of Highways is responsible for administration of the design, construction, and maintenance of the national and interprovincial routes, while the provincial roads and city streets are administered by local governments. However, in 1971, the director was assigned the maintenance responsibility for rural roads, while reconstruction of rural roads remained a provincial function.

Efforts of the Director General to repair and maintain the highway system were halted by the enemy. Even if the government had been successful, it is doubtful that a satisfactory level of highway maintenance could have been attained; the increased weight and volume of heavy military vehicles would have quickly negated the Vietnamese effort. In 1966 Army engineer troops began to reopen highways and rebuild bridges to support tactical and logistic traffic. The engineer force was probably adequate, but its effort was limited by other priority missions.

In early 1967 the idea of a formal highway restoration program, initially utilizing troops and later civilian contractors, was conceived as the result of a combined effort on the part of the government of

Vietnam, the United States Agency for International Development, and the Military Assistance Command, Vietnam. The combined Central Highways and Waterways Coordination Committee (CENCOM) was formed to establish priorities of restoration, to develop standards of construction, and to fund actual construction. CENCOM was comprised of representatives from the Vietnamese General Staff, the Agency for International Development, the Directorate of Highways, the Military Assistance Command, and the Marine Director of Public Works. The chairman was the Chief of Staff of the Vietnamese Joint General Staff. The program envisioned the eventual restoration and upgrading of approximately 4,075 kilometers of highway, which the committee considered essential in support of military operations, to stimulate economic development, and to accelerate the pacification program by opening up rural areas. The information of the combined committee permitted the development of a national restoration program in consonance with military campaign plans.

In April 1968 the Agency for International Development published a formal announcement of the transfer of the highway mission, with the exception of secondary road projects, to the MACV Director of Construction. Included in the transfer were the Nui Sap Quarry operation, the National Highway Training School, the Suoi Lo Maintenance and Repair Parts Activity, and nineteen USAID engineers. The Director of Construction then organized a Lines of Communications Division to advise the Vietnamese Director General of Highways and to co-ordinate the massive contractor and troop effort involved in the highway restoration program. The Lines of Communications Division organized five district highway advisory detachments to correspond with the highway directorate's field organization. The detachments' primary mission was to advise the Vietnamese District Engineer and his staff.

The advisory mission was established as a three-phase operation. Phase I was to effect transition of the ongoing organization from USAID control to MACV. Phase II was to substantially increase the advisory effort available to the Vietnamese District Engineer. Phase III would be the transferral of the responsibility back to the Agency for International Development in 1971. The objective of the highway restoration program was to upgrade designated highways over a four-year period to adopted standards and in accordance with established priorities.

Construction standards followed the criteria established by the American Association of State Highway officials. The standards which were identified by letters A through F had a design life for a Class A road of twenty years down to ten years for Classes C or D.

Pavement structure design procedures were standardized using estimated traffic factors to approximate a twenty-year design life. Each class of highway had specific geometrics. Cross sections of each class are shown in *Chart 7*. The Class F highway was an innovation introduced by MACV's Director of Construction. This class made maximum use of the existing French-constructed highway and based its

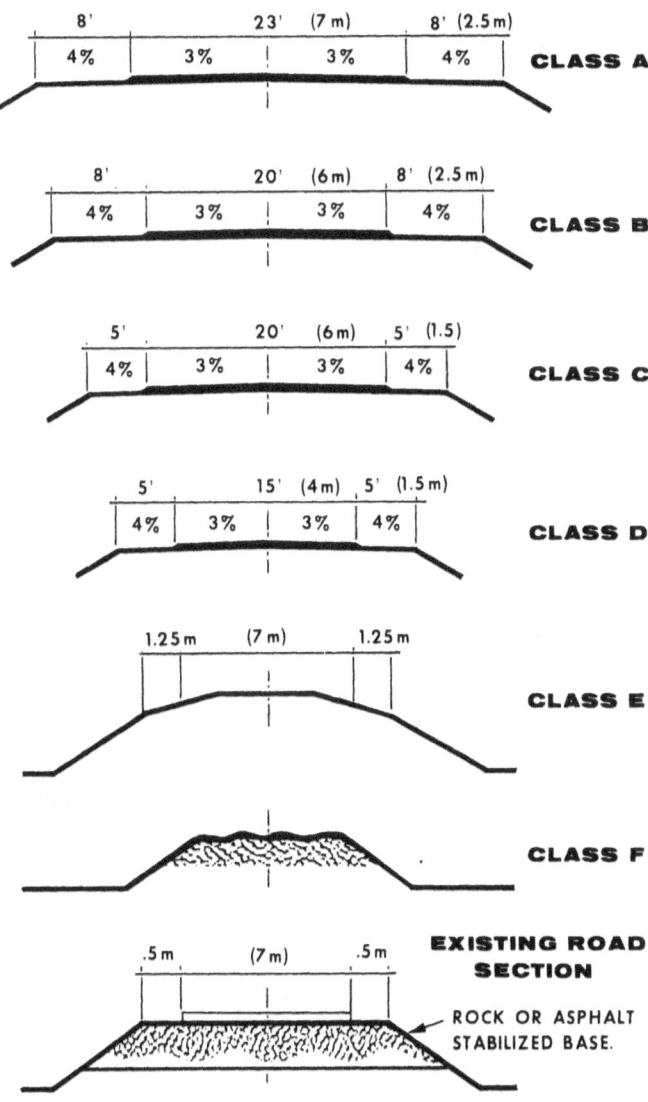

CHART 7—MACV ROAD CROSS SECTIONS

alignment on the existing embankment. Essentially this class highway called for laying a rock or asphalt stabilized base over the existing highway and a widening of the traveled way, or actual road less shoulders, to seven meters. The entire surface would then be paved with an asphaltic concrete. Design life would not be specified. The Class F highway would be constructed extensively in the delta, thus minimizing embankment and realignment requirements and speeding up the highway restoration program there.

Sixteen engineer battalions undertook the U.S. Army's portion of the highway restoration program. The work force was composed largely of construction battalions; however, an average of three combat battalions augmented with equipment companies were engaged in the program at any given time. Although restoration of the roads was their main task, construction units frequently received orders to support combat units or were given other priority missions. Unit commanders tried to construct all highways in accordance with established priorities, but on many occasions combat engineers called on them for help and missions were shifted.

To carry out the program, units had to establish base camps along the routes to be upgraded. This requirement made it necessary to devote a part of the available manpower to base camp and industrial site construction. Quarries and asphalt plants had to be established, construction routes and security had to be maintained, and that drew off more manpower.

To maintain construction schedules, a vast amount of material had to be procured and transported to the construction sites. Initially the demand on procurement and transport was light, since construction was centered near large U.S. logistics bases. But as demands increased and construction forces moved farther away from the larger bases, a tremendous burden was placed on the entire supply system. To reduce the number of times material was handled, the Engineers attempted to ship directly from supply points to users. Stocks of cement, asphalt, and culvert material began to dwindle rapidly. As material shortages threatened delay, logisticians pulled out all the stops and attempted to meet demands any way possible. Critically needed items were improvised or borrowed from other services.

In 1966 there was an acute shortage of rock in III and IV Corps areas. At that time there were only two sources for crushed rock—a contractor-operated quarry near Saigon University and the quarries thirty miles away at Vung Tau. Because Vung Tau had no connecting roads, the rock produced there was used there with only small quantities being shipped by barge to the Long Binh area. The need for rock was so urgent that a special "buy" of rock was made from a Korean contractor who shipped rock all the way from quarries in Korea.

When the first shipment of rock arrived in Saigon, headaches really began. Customs, harbor, and lighterage problems combined to produce lengthy delays and creeping costs. A scheme was finally devised whereby the rock was loaded into "smaller craft" at Saigon for the trip to Thu Duc, to be unloaded there by heavy equipment into trucks for the short haul to Long Binh. A crane with a two-cubic-yard clamshell, or heavy steel scoop, was positioned at Thu Duc to unload the rock. There was considerable consternation as the small craft loaded with rock began arriving at Thu Duc. The small craft were hundreds of sampans—the largest nearing twenty feet stem to stern and loaded to within six inches of freeboard. The weight and size of the clamshell would have sunk them easily. Reluctantly, conveyors and hand labor were used to bring the rocks ashore. Stockpiles from which the clamshell could operate slowly grew on the beach. Since this method of supplying rock was rather nightmarish, the first shipload was also the last. The contract was terminated.

The entire highway restoration program was originally scheduled for completion by 1974. But because of the tactical and economic importance of the program, General Westmoreland directed the Army to have the majority of the roadwork finished by 1971. The principal obstacle was the shortage of construction equipment. The solution was for the Army to purchase high-production commercial equipment to augment the standard items used by engineer units. In mid-1968 the U.S. Army in Vietnam, in conjunction with the Army Engineer Construction Agency and the 18th and 20th Engineer Brigades, studied the equipment problem from all angles. The study resulted in a recommended list of commercial construction equipment that would be needed to meet the target completion date of December 1971. In determining the type of equipment required, specialists developed seven general categories and assigned each category a rating reflecting its importance to the success of the project.

In mid-1968 the rock production capabilities of both engineer brigades received a thorough analysis including actual and anticipated assets. These capabilities were then compared with all other rock requirements. From this study it became apparent that additional rockcrushers would be required to complete the road program by the specified time. Eight 250-tons-per-hour (TPH), readily portable, crushing plants were selected and included in the equipment purchase order. High-volume crushers were considered the key to the success of the project. As these crushers reached Vietnam,

ROCK-CRUSHING OPERATION, *essential to virtually all phases of construction.*

they replaced the lower capacity 75-TPH plants. The newer 250-TPH plant was as portable as the 75-TPH plant but easier to operate and maintain, produced at least three times as much rock, and required fewer operators. Although the larger plant was designed with emphasis on high-volume base rock production, the all-electric plant had the capability of producing well-graded aggregates. The rapid rate of road improvement in 1969 was possible only because six 225-TPH rockcrushers had arrived from CONUS depot stocks. These crushers played a major part in the program until the Military Construction 250-TPH crushers arrived. These crushers required only one operator whereas the 75-TPH needed three. As the new crushers arrived in the theater, many of the 75-TPH units which were not economically repairable were turned in. The operators previously required for the 75-TPH crushers were then available for other equipment.

The scarcity of rock-drilling equipment also hindered progress. Engineer units had far too few drills capable of keeping up with the increased demand for rock. Reinforcements in drilling equipment were necessary to feed the eight 250-TPH crushers and the six 225-TPH crushers. To meet the demand, thirty-six track drills and 600-cubic-foot-per-minute air compressors were added to the equipment purchase list.

Requirements for hauling rock within the quarries were met by

Rock Drill *operating on quarry face.*

purchasing one hundred 15-cubic-yard Euclid dump trucks in 1967. But to load the Euclids, feed the crushers, and stockpile aggregate, twenty-nine 6-cubic-yard tractor shovels were needed. Far simpler to operate and faster and easier to maintain, each of these units could replace two 40-ton shovels. Furthermore, an experienced heavy-equipment operator could become reasonably proficient on the machine in a matter of several days, whereas many months were required for him to become equally proficient on a crane shovel.

To augment existing trucks, 226 twelve-cubic-yard, hydraulically operated, dump trucks were selected for purchase. Under comparable conditions, these trucks have twice the capacity of the military 5-ton dump truck and were requested specifically to haul large quantities of base rock and asphaltic concrete on medium to long hauls over improved roads.

The earth compaction equipment used by engineer units was not in scale with the projected construction rate of 774 kilometers a year. Compactors capable of doing more work in less time were urgently needed to augment the equipment in the construction battalions. The purchase of sixty commercial heavy-duty compactors certainly increased the capabilities of our engineer units.

The concept of the road program also included the rapid placing of pavement. In addition to strengthening and protecting the roadbed, paving would make mine emplacement more difficult for the enemy. To supplement existing military equipment and to speed up the over-all paving rate, six asphalt pavers and fourteen asphalt

SHEEPSFOOT ROLLER *compacting a runway extension at Bu Dop airstrip.*

distributors were ordered. To redirect and channel the runoff which results from the torrential monsoon rains, seven asphalt curb extruders were included in the order. These were put to use primarily in the Central Highlands, but were also used to manufacture curb and gutter systems for villages and towns in other areas.

To keep culvert installation ahead of over-all road building, and at the same time assure quality construction, hand compactors were requested to speed up culvert backfilling and compaction operations. Twelve backhoes were also added to the equipment list to aid in the placement of culverts and excavation in restricted areas. Thousands of man-hours required for hand excavation of culverts and trenches and many hours of equipment time on crane mounted shovels or clamshells were saved by the backhoes.

The addition of commercial cement mixers had been requested to accelerate the construction of concrete abutments, deck slabs, and approach slabs for bridges along the roads. This equipment was designed to minimize the labor force needed for concrete work. There were approximately 675 new bridges with an average span length of forty feet to be constructed to satisfy immediate tactical requirements. The type of bridge planned required approximately

165 cubic yards of concrete per bridge. The small 16S cement mixers were being replaced by central batch plants and transit mixers which greatly reduced the stockpiling requirements and the man-hours needed to produce the concrete required for each bridge. By carrying a dry mix in the transit mixers, more than one bridge could be worked on at one time. In the long run, both production and maintenance man-hours were significantly reduced.

In the Mekong Delta all rock and other conventional material for road and other construction had to be imported. Crushed rock produced at quarries in the upper regions of the country moved by barge into the delta for the road construction program. Barge offloading facilities were constructed, and an Army Engineer Hydrographic Survey team charted many of the canals of the delta to develop water transportation routes. To reduce cost the use of a lime-cement stabilized base or subbase in lieu of a conventional base was planned for all delta road construction. Elsewhere in Vietnam the use of stabilization techniques was planned to reduce requirements in areas where little rock was available. The procurement of sophisticated stabilization equipment capable of mixing stabilizing agents, such as cement, calcium chloride, and emulsified asphalt with aggregate, was considered vital for project completion. A total of nine 300-TPH stabilization plants and three self-propelled stabilization machines were requested. These plants represented a revolutionary change in theater construction methods.

While the addition of commercial construction equipment increased production, the redeployment of engineer battalions, which began in September 1970, reduced U.S. troop strengths below that needed to meet the December 1971 completion date. To partially offset the troops losses, some engineer battalions were augmented with local labor. Initially the local laborers were used for unskilled or semiskilled duties. However, by the end of 1970, the Vung Tau quarry was predominantly staffed with Vietnamese labor; several dump truck platoons employed Vietnamese drivers; and carpenter prefab and bridge deck prefab yards were almost entirely Vietnamese operated. In early 1971 an all-Vietnamese asphalt concrete paving train was being organized.

The secondary road program, as it neared completion, was a significant incentive to the development of Vietnam, particularly in the areas of agriculture, economy, and mobility. This diversified highly productive program permitted U.S. and Vietnamese engineers to work side by side and eventually developed a proficiency in Vietnamese units for both construction and maintenance of the road system.

The stimulus to agriculture was particularly pronounced in

previously evacuated areas. Construction of a secondary road presupposed a relatively secure area, which was ripe for resettlement. While the road was not necessary for the movement of relocated people and their few personal belongings, it was crucial to the establishment of a market for their crops. A difference of a few miles and a few hundred feet in elevation often resulted in differing climate and soil conditions which dictate the primary production of tea and manioc, rather than rice; hence the need for easily accessible markets in other than the settlers' own village.

The opening or reconstruction of secondary and rural roads was recognized by General Westmoreland and pacification officials as critical to the pacification and economic growth of Vietnam. The tremendous advances in pacification in the delta, for example, were a direct result of the road building program.

The railway system in Vietnam was originally constructed by the French between 1902 and 1936. Immediately after the Geneva Agreement in 1954, the Republic of Vietnam mobilized its financial, technical, and labor resources under the newly formed semiautonomous railway agency, the Vietnam Railway System, and began the reconstruction of its road between Saigon and Dong Ha near the 17th parallel. By August 1959 the reconstruction of the main line and branch lines was completed, except for the Loc Ninh branch. The United States government through the embassy's Operating

SCRAPERS PREPARE A RIGHT OF WAY *before crushed rock is dumped.*

Mission assigned a railway adviser to Vietnam in 1957 at the request of the Vietnamese government.

From 1960 to 1964 the Vietnamese Railway System operated scheduled freight and passenger trains on the entire line, transporting approximately half a million tons of cargo and four million passengers annually. In 1962 the U.S. military assigned security advisers to the Vietnamese Military Rail Security Forces. During this period the system continued to upgrade its entire organization by modernizing shop facilities, mechanizing track maintenance, changing motive power from steam to diesel-electric, and replacing rolling stock with modern equipment. The United States assisted with commodity grants amounting to $12 million and a development loan of $7.8 million. The Australian government furnished ten modern passenger cars valued at U.S. $900,000.

In November 1964, typhoons Joan and Iris, the worst to strike Vietnam in sixty-five years, did considerable damage to the railway system and, with unabated Viet Cong sabotage, the railway was severed in many places with operations restricted to five separated segments.

In 1966 the U.S. government through the Agency for International Development pledged further support in commodities provided that the Vietnamese took the initiative to secure and reopen the rail system. This action was sanctioned by the U.S. military, which acquired and brought into the country two hundred rail cars and ten switching locomotives to supplement the fleet of Vietnamese rolling stock for the handling of military cargo.

This second reconstruction effort began in December 1966 and progressed in those areas where security was re-established. During this second reconstruction period the U.S. government assisted with U.S. $11 million in commodity grants. The system reopened 340 kilometers of main line in areas where security was restored. The government subsidized the road for this reconstruction in the amount of Vietnamese $211 million, in addition to the subsidy for operations or sabotage.

The railway contributed significantly to the war effort, the pacification program, and the economic growth of South Vietnam. For instance, a considerable amount of the rock aggregate used in the construction of the Tuy Hoa and Phu Cat airfields, as well as Route 1 and other highways, was transported by rail. As of early 1971 the railroad was in operation in three separate areas with approximately 60 percent, or 710 kilometers, of the 1,240 kilometers of main line and branch line track in use. The longest run, approximately 400 kilometers, from Song Long Song to Phu Cat handled a number of rock trains daily for highway construction work. Military

VIETNAMESE ENGINEERS *drive piles for a bridge span near Qua Giang with new American equipment.*

cargo from Qui Nhon and Cam Ranh Bay still moves by rail to Phu Cat, Tuy Hoa, Ninh Hoa, Nha Trang, and Phan Rang. The system also transports approximately 11,000 passengers weekly over this line. Another segment of 103 kilometers from Hue to Da Nang, which was reopened in January 1969, has averaged approximately 2,000 tons of cargo and 1,500 passengers a week. The remaining 80 kilometers from Saigon to Xuan Loc, serving the Thu Duc industrial area and the Long Binh and Newport military complex, play an important role in transporting civilian and military cargo. Operation of this line has eliminated a large number of truck runs from the congested streets of Saigon and the Bien Hoa Highway. Three round-trip passenger trains operate daily over this section of the road, transporting an average of 40,000 commuters a week.

The economics of moving cargo by rail, plus the advantage of releasing trucks for work in the provinces, made rail traffic attractive to the Vietnamese Army and U.S. military.

The entire road program, both the rail and vehicular systems, has undergone a tremendous change as has Vietnam. The bridge reconstruction portion of the road program involved the building of approximately five hundred bridges totaling over 30,000 meters. During mid-1968, Army engineers were constructing highways to MACV standards at an equivalent rate of 285 kilometers per year. At the same time, they were building bases and supporting combat operations—including land clearing, tactical roads, tactical airfields, landing zones, and fire bases. Road construction has continually been paced by crushed rock production and rock-hauling capability. The Army relied on the contractor's crushers for 38 percent of the 180,000 cubic yards of rock required monthly to maintain a construction rate of 285 kilometers per year in 1968.

Before a $49 million fund cut was imposed by the Department of Defense, in mid-1970 goals were assigned for the highway restoration program.

Vietnamese Army responsibility ...	165 km.
Contractor responsibility	988 km.
U.S. Army troop responsibility	2,520 km.
U.S. Navy responsibility	430 km.
Total	4,103 km.

As of 17 October 1970, the revised highway restoration program was 63 percent complete with 2,297 kilometers of pavement completed out of a total of 3,660 kilometers. As a result of the fund cuts and program review, 442 kilometers of the 4,103 kilometers CENCOM Program were deferred. The Vietnamese engineers accepted responsibility for improving 353 additional kilometers in the program. The revised program totals and goals were as follows:

	Revised Program	Pavement Completed	Percent Completed
Vietnamese Army responsibility	518 km.	10 km.	2
Contractor responsibility	902 km.	715 km.	79
U.S. Army troop responsibility	1,853 km.	1,195 km.	64
U.S. Navy responsibility	387 km.	387 km.	100
Total	3,660 km.		

As primary and secondary roads were built or improved, displaced refugees settled along these roads, constructed new homes, and tilled the land. Commercial traffic traveled back and forth with decreasing fear as the area became generally pacified. Land clearing to remove vegetation along roads and in other selected areas, thus denying the enemy ambush sites and sanctuaries for resupply, also accomplished what repeated infantry operations could not. And as the rail service was improved and security provided, the demand increased. During 1970 cargo transported by rail climbed 15 percent over 1969 (from 530,000 to 610,000 metric tons). The net ton-kilometer evaluation increased 100 percent from 1969 to 1970 (from 24 million to 48 million net ton-kilometers). The number of passengers transported by rail increased 40 percent from 1969 to 1970 (from 1.75 million to 2.4 million). The net results of the combined program have not yet proved their greatest worth, but are well along the way. I consider the road development program the single most effective and important development program undertaken by American effort in Vietnam.

CHAPTER IX

Construction Logistics

The orderly time-phased buildup of logistics support with tactical operations, as envisioned in Army logistical doctrine, obviously did not occur in Vietnam. Moreover, there was no meaningful consumption or other experience data upon which to base support estimates. Nevertheless, the effective support of combat operations was mandatory, and this meant an influx of mammoth quantities of supplies of every description well before the availability of either a logistic base or an adequate logistical organization. A system of "push" supply was developed as an expedient, with supplies literally pushed into the theater on a best estimate basis until such time as normal supply procedures could be established. Consequently, the logistic base was literally engulfed in a sea of supply which would clog both storage areas and supply machinery for years afterward. Even as late as 1968 the ill-fated corner of Long Binh Post known as Area 208 could accurately be described as a disaster area. To further complicate matters, supply not only arrived in the wrong mix and quantities but often arrived at the wrong place. The fluidity of the tactical situation and a lack of supply and transport control resulted in the depositing of tons of material hundreds of miles from the intended customer.

The logistics establishment in Vietnam in 1964 was minimal, at least relative to later requirements, and highly fragmented. It actually consisted of some sixteen different systems which developed in a more or less hit-and-miss fashion with co-ordination accomplished essentially by informal working agreements. This conglomerate structure supported the contingents of six nations: the United States, South Vietnam, New Zealand, Australia, the Republic of the Philippines, and the Republic of China. The Republic of Vietnam provided some support, while the United States provided food, individual equipment, administrative transportation, hospitalization, and maintenance and repair parts support. This of course excluded the input of military supply and equipment for the Vietnamese Army, which was accomplished through the military advisory structure.

No one organization had full responsibility for logistics support, which was provided largely on a case-by-case basis. For example, the Headquarters Support Activity, Saigon, and the MACV headquarters commandant operated parallel supply lines in support of U.S. advisers until 1966. Four different systems furnished repairs, and each of the services had its own medical supply system operating on a "stovepipe" basis to CONUS. Certain services, such as port shipper functions, and a so-called logistics co-ordinator were assigned to each of the corps tactical zones. However, even his functions were limited to billeting, mess operation, generator repair, and the like.

With the continued growth of American and other contingents, it became apparent that this minimal and fragmented logistics support system would not work and that a general overhaul was needed. The logical approach was seen as focusing support as much as possible within a single command, and in the latter part of 1964 Military Assistance Command proposed that an Army Logistical Command be introduced into the country. At least major functions could be combined under a single command, reducing duplication, ensuring co-ordination and control, and thus providing better logistical support. The 1st Logistical Command, then at Fort Hood, Texas, was designated to fill this role. The command was originally activated in May 1965, with an authorized headquarters strength of 329 personnel. The enormous expansion of the 1st Logistical Command's responsibilities was reflected in the size of the organization in mid-1969. At that time the command's strength was approximately 50,000 military and 30,000 civilian personnel, and it supported over half a million U.S. and other Free World forces in Vietnam. However, the evolution of the logistics system resulted from continual command and management problems inherent in providing logistical support to all U.S. and Free World contingents.

From 1965 to 1966, the sixteen different support systems managed by separate services were pulled together. The command would manage all logistics and support functions for the Army except for aviation supply and maintenance support and engineer construction.

Development, consolidation, and refinement continued into 1967. The logistics structure of the earlier years was modified to provide more intensive management in key areas. Engineer facilities engineering was placed under the newly formed U.S. Army Engineer Construction Agency, Vietnam. Port and depot development continued and were highlighted by the completion of Newport, the modern military port facility built on the Saigon River at the cost of over $50 million. Modern computer equipment was installed in the 14th Inventory Control Center to attempt to bring some order out of the supply chaos in the depot stock inventory. The major problem encountered was the tremendous influx of supplies which went over the beaches and through the ports flooding the depots under a massive sea of matériel and equipment much of which was later found to be unneeded. Push supplies and duplicate requisitions of thousands of tons of cargo piled up in the depots, unrecorded and essentially lost to the supply system. In the latter part of 1967, control was slowly established over the requisitioning system through the use of automation; the flow of unneeded supplies abated somewhat.

The 14th Inventory Control Center, Vietnam, was deployed in December 1965 and was later equipped with third generation computer equipment to manage USARV's total depot assets. Special projects were established to comb through all the depots to identify, count, and pick up stock assets which had lost their supply identity during the "push" period. Thousands of tons of supplies and matériel were identified, permitting the cancellation of millions of dollars worth of requisitions. Still more thousands of tons of supplies were returned to offshore depots for redistribution. The fundamental deficiency was in the gross inadequacy of the management information system. While many logistic deficiencies were the natural result of human errors made under pressure, the majority could be ultimately traced to a lack of timely, accurate, well analyzed, and well co-ordinated logistics intelligence. The information system, from bottom echelon to top and back, was essentially a horse and buggy rig applied to a fantastic array of data. It depended for the most part upon the manual development of input data, transmitted by telephone, liaison officer, or written reports; it was a laborious manual affair. Finally, hand-annotated charts were prepared and presented to the commander by Vu-Graph display. Harvesting and analyzing masses of presumably "real time" data through these procedures are akin to nailing jelly to the wall with sometimes similar results.

The major problems in defining construction needs in Vietnam had resulted from an inadequate planning capability in the Army and Navy components of the Military Assistance Command headquarters. Makeshift staffs were forced to plan while elsewhere other plans were already afoot. Confusion and delays resulted. Many of the largest installations, originally established for no more than initial homesteads, grew from very small bases. Comprehensive long-range planning was made more difficult by the continued incremental increase in force size and structure, which only further added to logistics headaches.

The data published in Technical Manuals 5-301, 5-302, and 5-303 was originally gathered to provide base planning information.

These manuals represented a compilation of staff guidance for ordering and constructing installations and individual facilities in the theater of operations. Collectively known as the Engineer Functional Components System, or EFCS, the information was compiled to make base building a rather simple task. The data available in these three technical manuals could be used in either of two ways. Individual buildings or facilities could be constructed using the plans provided and ordering material from the bills of material found in the last volume, or an entire installation could be ordered by placing a single requisition in the supply system.

Since all the structures in the EFCS were wooden and designed for a temperate as opposed to a tropical climate, if individual structures were built using the plans and bills of material provided—with certain modifications—everything went well. Certain items would not be ordered, and other federal stock numbers would be used to order slightly different materials. For example, tar paper for roofing would be replaced with corrugated steel roofing, and more screening would have to be ordered for a tropical hut. However, if the material for an entire installation were ordered by requesting that installation by number on only one requisition, an entire bill of materials including insulation, roofing felt, and tar paper would arrive. And how this bulk construction material

VIETNAMESE CONSTRUCTION WORKERS *erect a tropicalized hut at Tan Son Nhut.*

arrived was an entirely different matter. The palletized lumber, crates of nails, and electrical and plumbing fixtures were shipped by the Army Materiel Command. Lumber for one project looks like lumber for any other project. Needless to say, many facilities were diverted before they ever became facilities. Identification of construction matériel assets was a problem of considerable magnitude. Materials identified by federal stock numbers did not present a problem and were managed as provided for by current supply directives. However, bulk construction buys, especially electrical and plumbing supplies and other special purpose procurement items, were identified by special project codes and consisted of items which were not, in approximately 60 percent of the total, identified by federal stock numbers. Shipments were made up of several packages placed inside a large crate which in turn was identified with a three-letter project code. In some instances the crates were stored by project code, and the individual items were never recorded on stock record cards. In other instances the crates were opened, and each item was stored according to either federal stock number or federal supply class without regard to project code or funding source. Those items which were not identified by a federal stock number were assigned a depot number for storage and identification purposes. Unfortunately, in most instances each depot assigned a different number to the same item, and any attempt at accomplishing a total inventory of nonstock numbered items was doomed to failure.

Construction materials for use in I Corps Tactical Zone were supplied, with few exceptions, by the U.S. Navy. Materials for II, III, and IV Corps Tactical Zones were stored in four depots located at Qui Nhon, Cam Ranh Bay, Long Binh, and Vung Tau. Each of these depots had an engineer construction materials yard operated by civilian contractors. Bulk purchase assets were, in general, distributed with approximately 25 percent to Qui Nhon, 26 percent to Cam Ranh Bay, 33 percent to Long Binh, and 16 percent to Vung Tau. Army Operations and Maintenance (OMA) assets were stored according to demand experience or in forecast amounts for each individual depot. Certain items such as lumber, asphalt products, and cement were stored and issued under the common stockpile concept to increase supply flexibility and matériel availability. These items were stored in a common location at each depot and issued according to immediate requirements without regard to funding sources.

Accountability for construction material assets in storage depots was a responsibility of the 1st Logistical Command. Construction assets received for storage were entered on an account for the item in question. Receiving engineer construction units were required to charge issued materials against an approved construction directive and report material consumption as completed work "in place." Operations and Maintenance construction materials were accounted for in much the same manner except that materials were accounted for by completed individual job order requests. Errors in accounting procedures were common. Improper identification of incoming shipments, manual errors in posting stock records, cancellation of projects before completion with assets diverted to other projects of higher priority, inability of units to return unused assets to depot stocks, and the absence of a uniform inventory control system at all levels resulted in questionable over-all accounting for construction materials. Accountability and balances were maintained on separate stock record cards. The concept provided for loaning assets to either account, when required to prevent work stoppage, and repayment in kind when "due-in" assets were received.

When adequate stocks were available in the supporting storage depot and the stock records indicated an asset's availability, requisitioning units experienced excellent supply response. If, however, the supporting depot was out of stock and its records indicated assets due in, the requesting unit could expect not to have its requirements satisfied from available stocks located in another depot. The passing of unfilled construction material requisitions to the Inventory Control Center for referral to other depots was considered an exception to normal practice. One program, Construction Materials-Special Handling, operated by the 1st Logistical Command, was successful in reducing procurement lead time provided only that the required materials were air transportable.

By late 1966 use of the Engineer Functional Components System was discontinued. The system had been found unsatisfactory for providing matériel support on a long-term basis, design criteria were incompatible with theater demands, and building and maintenance forecasts were not possible. The predicting of requirements for construction materials involved a summation of materials required to complete programed construction based on projected manpower and equipment resources, and this was not provided for in the Engineer Functional Components System.

Requests for materials required for new construction projects were based on estimated construction projects for a given six- to twelve-month period. Requests were submitted to the 1st Logistical Command in the form of Construction Material Requirement Letters, which were used for bulk procurement and to assign material storage at preselected depots in specified quantities. Bulk material purchase requests valued at $45 million were submitted between

July 1967 and May 1968. This amount was not, however, anywhere near the sum of construction material expenses.

Operating and maintenance budgets and funds were usually determined by 1st Logistical Command based on data as it accumulated at matériel storage depots. Wide demand fluctuations, however, forced 1st Logistical Command to resort to forecasting for future requirements. Demands for cement, asphalt, bridge timbers, and structural steel generally defied prediction.

Once in the country, construction assets, with certain exceptions, were placed on the list of command-controlled items to provide some measure of intensified management. Requisitioning procedures were developed wherein each requisition was to be annotated with the appropriate construction directive number and account coding before the storage depot would honor the document. Operating and maintenance assets were not placed under any type of special control. They were ordered, received, stored, and issued in accordance with current basic supply regulations. Control of issues was not very effective in that the authority to requisition and quantities involved were based primarily on the honesty of the requisitioner.

Identifying and segregating materials for purposes of fund accounting in an active theater is almost impossible, and if accounting must be done it should be done at the procuring agency level. Accountability for all funded materials and installed equipment should have ceased with their shipment from CONUS or the country where they were purchased. Instead, identification of construction material assets became a problem of increasing magnitude. Materials identified by federal stock number did not present a problem, but because of the type of construction going on, about 60 percent of the total items were not covered by stock numbers. Since each depot had created its own accounting system for these items, no over-all correlation of accounting was possible. Depots receiving requisitions for an out-of-stock item placed the requisitions on back order without referral to other depots where the stocks might be available.

In 1969 Major General Joseph M. Heiser, Jr., Commanding General, 1st Logistical Command, had occasion to report:

> We have massed at one time in Vietnam far too many thousands of tons of construction supplies to meet requirements of the construction program. It has been push requisitioned in terms of complete programs or to cover R&U requirements covering many months ahead. Thus the logistic system has become bogged down with supplies far greater than the immediate requirement necessitated. (A good example of this is the fact that we at one time had over two years' supply of M8A1 matting—this equaled approximately 180,000 short tons that were stored in our three major depots). This unnecessarily increases security requirements.

The combat zone is not the place to store equipment and supplies that are not essential . . . .

If there was an overabundance of construction materials in Vietnam at any time, the oversupply of repair parts was more of a problem than an asset. Parts were often lost somewhere in the supply system. The nonsupply of repair parts for construction equipment continued to account for two-thirds of the not operationally ready (NOR) rate. Worldwide, the NOR rate for construction equipment is 25 percent, of this parts supply (NORS) accounts for 16 percent and maintenance (NORM) for 9 percent. The NOR rate in Vietnam was worse during the early stages of the war for a wide variety of reasons.

Compared to other Army equipment, engineer machinery has a tremendously high rate of use. Nearly all construction units in

D-7 TRACTOR *working a borrow pit.*

Vietnam operated on a two-shift schedule, approximately twenty hours a day. While tanks may operate three or four hours a day, a D-7 tractor may be run twenty hours with little time out for maintenance. In order to keep the engineer equipment deadline rate at an acceptable low, a sizable maintenance reserve or "float" was required. The punishing environment in Vietnam, however, forced the number of items in the float to be raised as high as 30 percent of the total item assets.

Contributing to the maintenance problem was the high equipment density. For example, a light equipment company augmented each combat engineer battalion. This was quite a bit in excess of what had previously been considered normal. While the equipment augmentation was most helpful and desirable, it saturated the direct support maintenance people with work. On the other hand, the construction battalions had organic direct support maintenance capabilities. We have found that it is essential to have a similar capability if maintenance backlogs are to be avoided.

Since the prescribed load list, or the combat essential supplies and parts needed to sustain a unit in combat for at least fifteen days, is made up on the basis of experience, "demand" repair parts items usually constitute the greater part of the load list. But many engineer battalions were activated and deployed before they could develop demand data. Almost the same was true of maintenance units. Their authorized stockage lists were based on the equipment the unit supported. The repair parts stock level for each piece of equipment must be developed on the basis of prescribed items and demand-supported items. At least one direct support unit was deployed to Vietnam without its authorized stockage lists because no information was available on the equipment to be supported. This particular unit was ineffective for about a year. Subsequently, arrangements were made to furnish direct support units with parts for equipment known to have been shipped to Vietnam, thereby assuring at least a basic stock and permitting the theater to redistribute assets as necessary.

Resupply of parts was based essentially on a "purchase as needed" basis, since theater stocks were minimal. The low demand for individual construction equipment parts left many of these parts ineligible for stockage, and therefore they were not in depot stocks when requisitioned. Parts delivery lead times of six months to a year were not uncommon.

Maintenance difficulties were further caused by shortages of skilled mechanics and the locations of maintenance support units. Other problems were caused by the need to evacuate heavy construction equipment from jungle areas, requirements for heavy trailers, movement only by convoy, unexpected damage peculiar to jungle operations: radiator piercing, oil-pan rupture, and burned out engines. These problems were made worse by the many commissioned and noncommissioned officers who were not adequately trained in equipment maintenance. Problems were further aggravated by some officers who achieved low deadline rates through inadequate repair; lick and promise maintenance was good enough. In order to assist troop commanders, the USARV Engineer Command directed its brigades to start command maintenance management inspection teams and to establish both readiness assistance teams and a school for unit supply clerks.

Nearly $16 million worth of commercial construction equipment had been purchased with new construction funds in 1969 to hasten the construction and upgrading of more than 4,000 kilometers of Vietnamese highways. Contractor response in providing off-the-shelf equipment was more rapid than that experienced in the normal procurement of standard military items. Since most of this equipment was new to the Army, the contract provided that factory representatives would prepare the equipment for use and conduct operator training programs. A separate contract was awarded for civilian support to maintain the equipment, which included procurement of repair parts.

The concept of introducing commercial equipment into the Army in the field proved feasible in spite of some minor problems. For example, it was still exceedingly difficult to procure repair parts for nonstandard equipment. The procedure was to submit these repair parts requests to 1st Logistical Command for purchasing and contracting in CONUS and offshore procurement areas. There was no backup maintenance support for repair or repair parts of engineer nonstandard equipment beyond user level. The problems of special tools, and special repair and operator techniques, as well as additional requirements for operators and maintenance personnel for all echelons of repair remained.

To remedy the supply repair parts situation, a program called Red Ball Express was started in December of 1965 for all service equipment. It was originally designed to expedite the supply of repair parts for deadlined combat essential equipment; however, the program was later expanded to provide parts for equipment which was on the brink of maintenance failure. Red Ball provided the highest priority available for supply requisitioning and in that respect could be used to measure the effectiveness and performance of routine requisitioning procedures.

The initiator of the requisition assigned a document number to his requisition which was maintained throughout the system.

REPAIR PARTS FOR NONSTANDARD EQUIPMENT *like this rock crusher caused a continual logistics problem.*

This number was unique for Red Ball requisitions in that the document serial number was always in the 6,000 series. Thus, Red Ball requisitions were easily identifiable as the most urgent of requisitions. Since all requisitions were processed identically by machines, the Red Ball requisitions stood out in priority groupings.

The Logistics Control Office, Pacific, located at Fort Mason, California, controlled all requisitions. In addition to providing a positive control over Red Ball requisitions and ensuring prompt action on items affecting operational readiness, Red Ball procedures facilitated compilation of data in a form which was extremely useful to managers at all levels in that specific problems were highlighted.

Because there were so many nonmilitary items in use at the inception of the Red Ball system, requisitions by part number rather than federal stock number accounted for one-third of all requisitions received. This problem was significantly reduced. During the period April through June 1969, part number requisitions represented 8 percent of the total, or 3,289, individual requisitions. However, further analysis of these 3,289 items provided insight into more specific problem areas.

Both divisional and nondivisional engineer units experienced critical shortages of authorized equipment, particularly for earth moving, compaction, and water and asphalt distribution. Since the units were short authorized items, the maintenance float system for backup support was not developed for numerous essential construction items of equipment, with the result that the full construction potential of engineer units was not realized. These shortages can be attributed to loss of replacement requisitions somewhere between the using units and CONUS; lack of reconcilation between theater assets and assets as reflected by Army agencies; inadequate replacement factors; and the restrictions on the equipment purchase budget.

It is axiomatic that requirements for materials to support combat operations will tend to have priority over those needed for base development; however, a balanced receipt of both is required in any theater of war. In many cases in Vietnam, scarce items of construction materials were diverted from base development projects to support fire base and heliport construction. However, the large quantities of construction materials shipped into Vietnam during 1965 to 1967 alleviated much of the competition between claimants for combat support and service support. Not until a high-volume flow of construction materials was achieved could the constraint on base development be relieved.

The manner in which the fuel problem was finally solved aptly demonstrates the frustration inherent in Vietnamese construction logistics. If we consider that petroleum is one of the indispensable items without which a modern army cannot function, the confusion and waste inherent in the fuel supply problem should show what efforts were involved in support of the most essential construction.

At the beginning of 1965, the U.S. military had a limited petroleum logistic support capability in Vietnam. Three international oil companies, Esso, Shell, and Caltex, provided for virtually the entire oil supply system in Vietnam. Coastal, inland waterway, and overland transportation of bulk products, drummed fuels, and packaged lubricants were all provided by commercial suppliers. The contractors made all deliveries, including those to remote areas, although the facilities of these three companies were mainly situated at Nha Be, nine miles south of Saigon.

The contractor method of providing support had worked simply because U.S. military forces were in an advisory role. Total petroleum requirements were small and could be met through the use of existing commercial facilities. Before 1965 the small U.S. military orders in Southeast Asia were delivered in retail quantities, often in 55-gallon drums, to various locations in the field. Military requirements rose gradually from year to year until 1966. Through 1965 only a moderate expansion of commercial facilities was necessary to handle the slight increase in military requirements. During 1965, however, orders rose abruptly. It became necessary to decide on a course of action. Should we continue commercial support through the commercial distribution system, construct military storage, or use a combination of these?

At the time of the force buildup, the total oil and fuel storage in Vietnam amounted to approximately 1.6 million barrels, which was virtually all commercial. Approximately 80 percent of the storage was at the main terminals at Nha Be, 12 percent was at Da Nang, and the remainder was at other locations throughout Vietnam. None of these facilities could take on a fully loaded tanker. Nha Be, situated on a river, some thirty-six miles from the coast, had a draft limitation of twenty-six to twenty-seven feet. As a result, Nha Be had to be supplied by special shallow-draft tankers or by T–2 tankers loaded only to about 80 percent capacity. In the Da Nang area, installations at Lien Chieu had a draft of twenty-three feet and Nai Hon had a draft of fourteen feet. Lien Chieu could unload vessels of T–1 size, but Nai Hon could handle only barges that shuttled loads from tankers anchored in Da Nang Bay. Small terminals, such as Qui Nhon on the coast and Can Tho, Vinh Long, and Go Vap on inland waterways, were supplied by barge from Nha Be.

Initial military support was provided by assault equipment. In the Army, Navy, and Marine Corps, this equipment consisted primarily of 10,000-gallon collapsible tanks, 4-inch rubber hose, and 350-gallon-per-minute pumps. The Army and Navy also used buoyant and bottom-laid pipelines for ship-to-shore transfer into assault storage tanks. This equipment was designed, however, for the assault phase of an operation and should have normally been replaced as the operations area moved inland.

Of primary importance to Air Force operations were the R–1 portable hydrant fueling systems, which were 50,000-gallon collapsible tanks capable of servicing two aircraft at the rate of 300 gallons per minute. In January 1965, twenty-five of these systems were in Air Force inventories throughout the world. As operations in Vietnam expanded, they were all committed in Southeast Asia.

Early in 1965, evidence clearly pointed to the eventual exhaustion of commercial capabilities in the area. Although industry was expanding moderately, the expansion would not be sufficient to meet the additional needs of the military. Additional action was therefore necessary to provide the required support capability. Early in 1965 the policy for Vietnam called for continued reliance on commercial support. Admiral Felt hoped that under this policy industry would construct additional petroleum facilities in Vietnam for military purposes. To encourage civilian efforts, the Defense Fuel Supply Center issued on 17 May 1965 a request for proposals. Replies were not responsive for two reasons. Commercial storage already in being was far more than adequate for any foreseeable civilian demand after the end of hostilities, and the economic and physical hazards involved limitations for expansion. In view of these unattractive features, industry was reluctant to invest more in POL facilities.

In July 1965 Admiral Sharp, the new Commander in Chief, Pacific, recognizing the limitations of commercial support and the necessity for augmenting or replacing the commercial system, made specific assignments of responsibilities for support to the component commands. The Army was assigned support responsibility south of the Chu Lai area—this assignment covered the II, III, and IV Corps areas. The Navy was assigned support responsibility from Chu Lai to the Demilitarized Zone. The Air Force was assigned support responsibilities at airfields primarily designated for Air Force use.

Facilities ashore were so limited that floating storage was required during the early stages of the buildup. Continuation of this expensive practice was unfortunately necessary. Most of the problem was directly related to a lack of adequate American-owned or American-controlled bulk fuel storage. Because of the lack of adequate military storage, reliance was placed on a commercial-military system. The Commander in Chief, Pacific Fleet, and Commander, Service Forces, Pacific, recognized the problem and gave the highest priority to remedial construction and therefore diverted still more engineers. In 1965 the limited military permanent storage tanks in Vietnam were actually owned by the Vietnamese Air Force, and through local arrangements at Da Nang and Bien Hoa they were operated by the U.S. Air Force in support of all forces at those bases.

When the decision was made to provide a petroleum support capability in Vietnam, construction of storage facilities was controlled to the same extent as other Military Construction program projects and was subject to established policy and guidance. Storage was designed to augment or, if necessary, replace the existing commercial system. As the consumption of petroleum increased in Vietnam, the Army and Navy built semipermanent steel tankage for storage areas while the Air Force did the same for air bases. Initial storage was constructed to replace collapsible bladders at Da Nang, Chu Lai, Qui Nhon, An Khe, Tuy Hoa, Phan Rang, Nha Trang, Cam Ranh Bay, Vung Tau, Long Binh, and Can Tho. From late 1965 through 1966, military steel tankage and pipelines were constructed at all these areas as well as at Pleiku, Vung Ro Bay, Phan Thiet, and Soc Trang. The construction at Cam Ranh Bay was in

BLADDER FUEL CELLS *lie in sandbag revetments at the Cam Ranh POL facility.*

line with plans to make that location a major military redistribution facility. The primary source of semipermanent tankage became the 10,000-barrel-capacity bolted steel tanks in the inventory of the Navy Advanced Base Functional Component System. The Navy released 127 of these tanks to the Army and Air Force for use in Vietnam and Thailand.

The services did not have enough organic equipment or trained construction personnel to satisfy the heavy demand for constructing the needed port facilities, storage complexes, and distribution systems. Therefore, each to varying degrees had to rely on contractors to provide these facilities and systems.

By July 1966, U.S. forces were operating at more than fifty locations throughout Vietnam. Only twenty of those locations had a bulk fuel storage capability. The others used packaged stocks because requirements were small enough or because there was a lack of bulk fuel storage equipment.

In October 1966 the Joint Chiefs of Staff pointed out the need to construct more petroleum product storage facilities in Vietnam, stating that a storage capacity equal to thirty days' usage plus 10 percent would provide an average of about twenty days' supply on hand and that to maintain any semblance of a thirty-day level of stocks on hand about fifty days of storage capacity would be required. The storage situation in Vietnam was the subject of several messages between the Joint Chiefs of Staff and Admiral Sharp from

128   BASE DEVELOPMENT IN SOUTH VIETNAM

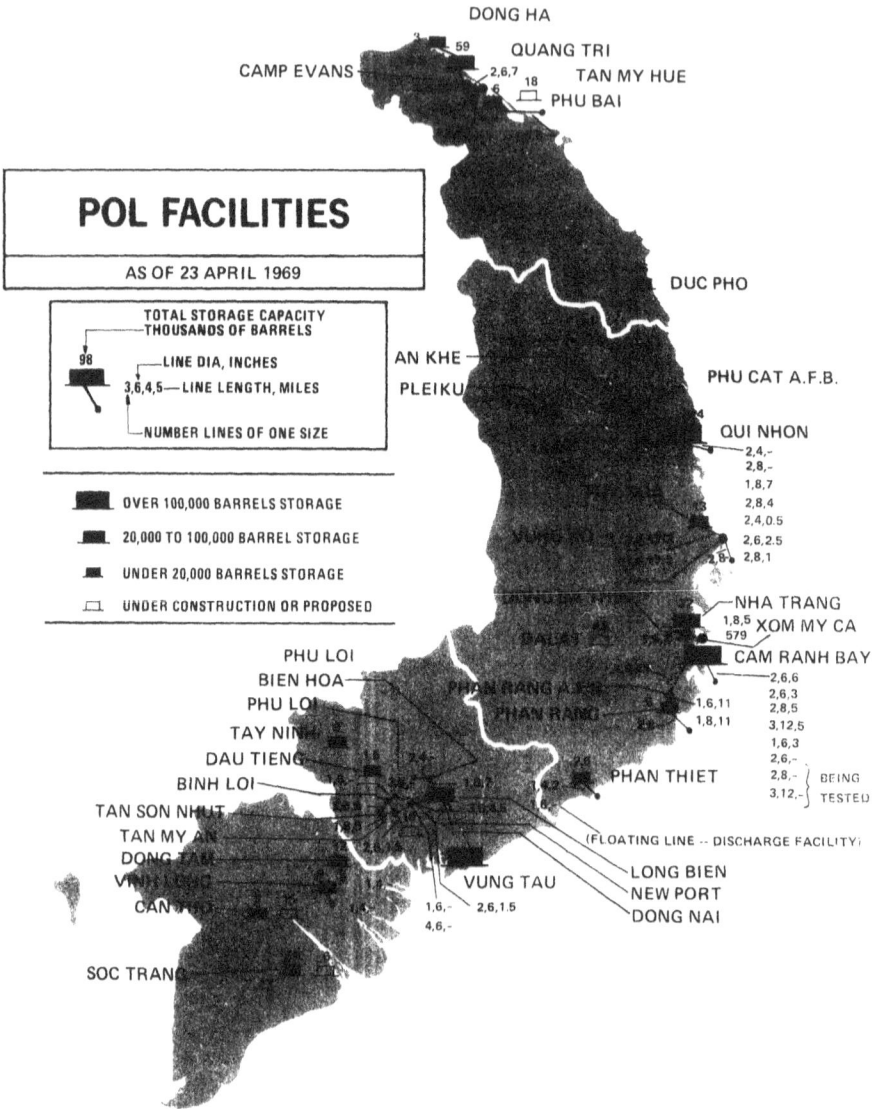

MAP 11

October 1966 to February 1967. Agreement was finally reached on a total construction goal of 4.4 million barrels of storage. While the differences in storage policy were being discussed, the military construction program for MACV never scheduled storage for more than 3.3 million barrels.

Shell Oil Company increased its petroleum complex at Da Nang with a mooring for T–5 tankers, 125,000 barrels of storage, and a pipeline connected with the military pipeline to the air base at Marble Mountain. After negotiations and construction delays, the facility at Da Nang was ready for operation by 1 January 1967. In the I Corps Tactical Zone, construction of tankage at Tan My was completed in 1967, and the Naval Support Activity assumed operation of the facility on 15 December 1967.

Since the demand continued to grow, storage capacity requirements continued to change, but actual storage capacity never reached planned for levels at most locations. Da Nang, with thirty-five days' storage, was the only major complex to equal or exceed the thirty-three days of storage desired by Admiral Sharp. Monthly consumption of oil products increased from 500,000 barrels per month in July 1965 to a high of more than 3 million barrels per month in 1968 while military storage rose to more than 2.6 million barrels. In the absence of sufficient permanent storage tanks, collapsible tanks (primarily 10,000-, 20,000-, and 50,000-gallon capacity) proved to be effective and highly useful. By October 1969 over $27 million worth of collapsible bladders had been shipped to Vietnam.

Since pipeline movement of fuel and oil was more efficient and

FUEL PIPELINES *stretched 270 miles through Vietnam.*

economical than highway transport when an area was secure enough for its use, a military construction program was undertaken, and by 1968 over 270 miles of pipeline were in use throughout Vietnam. (*Map 11*) However, commercial facilities in Vietnam remained vulnerable to the enemy. Particularly exposed to hostile action were the large commercial POL facilities at Nha Be near Saigon which, because of their contiguous locations, were particularly subject to the spread of fire and widespread damage by explosion. Tanker access facilities were also in jeopardy. Lien Chieu, across Da Nang Bay some eight miles northwest of the city and the second largest POL facility in early 1965, was very vulnerable to the enemy. It was the first of the commercial facilities to be badly damaged by the enemy when, in August 1965, he destroyed 60 percent of the tank-

TABLE 4—POL CAPABILITIES

LOCATION	STORAGE CAPACITY TOTAL THOUSANDS OF BARRELS			NUMBER AND CAPACITY OF TANKS IN PLACE THOUSANDS OF BARRELS	IN-LINE PUMP CAPACITY BARRELS/DAY	INCOMING PIPELINES NUMBER, DIA, (INCHES), LENGTH (MILES)
	IN PLACE	UNDER CONSTRUCTION	PROPOSED			
DONG HA	3.0				18,000	1,6,5
QUANG TRI	59.0			5-10 3-3	18,000	1,6,20
HUE					36,000	2,6,7
PHU BAI	6.0	18.0		2-3	18,000	1,6,11
CAMP EVANS					18,000	1,6,18
DUC PHO	16.0			5-3 1-1		
PHU CAT (AFB)					18,000	1,6,20
PLEIKU	59.0			3-3	18,000	1,6,63
AN KHE	69.0			5-10 5-3	18,000	1,6,53
QUI NHON	324.0			3-50 14-10 2-5 8-3	145,740	2,4,0.5 1,8,7 3,8,4
TUY HOA	13.0			4-3 2-0.5	43,000	1,6,17.2 1,8,17.2
NHA TRANG	72.0			6-10 4-2		
DALAT		4.5				
CAM RANH BAY	172 204 200 3			4-50 34-10 13-3	38,000 50,000 38,000 19,000 65,000	2,6,6 3,12,5 2,6,3 1,6,3 2,8,5
PHAN RANG		6.0		2-3	43,000	1,6,11 1,8,11
TAY NINH	9.0			3-3		
DAU TIENG	1.5			3-0.5	18,000	1,6,20
PHAN THIET	7.5			3-0.5	8,520	1,4,2
LONG BIEN	86.0			8-10 2-3	57,000 24,000	3,6,4.5 1,8,49
LONG BIEN (POWER PLANT) (VINHELL)	12.0				8,000	1,4,2
PHU LOI		9.0				
NEW PORT		10.0			38,000	2,6,1.5
VUNG TAU	250.0			3-50 10-10		
DONG TAM	12.0			4-3 2-0.5		
VINH LONG	9.0			2-3 3-1		
CAN THO BINH THUY	3.0		15.0	3-1		
SOC TRANG	2.5		6.0	2-1 1-0.5		

age. Since that time, there have been a number of attacks on commercial facilities including those at Nha Be, Tan Son Nhut, Qui Nhon, and Lien Chieu. The most significant losses amounted to $3.5 million at the Shell Nha Be Terminal. (*Table 4*)

Certainly early project planning is mandatory for logistics support, but when full planning for logistics is impossible—and not every contingency can be foreseen—backup programs should be available. To satisfy requirements like these and situations like Vietnam, the Department of Defense must maintain a prestructured base development planning group organized and staffed with experts that can respond far in advance of troop deployments. There must be specialists in electric power generation and distribution, port and airfield construction, POL storage and distribution, all areas of construction technology, and construction materials and equipment. If such a group had been available at the outset of the Vietnam buildup, some of the confusion in planning for base development logistics early in 1965 could have been avoided.

Technically, under current Army organization and supply doctrine, the engineer has no direct responsibility at the "wholesale" and procurement level of supply other than to forecast requirements for nonrecurring construction. In practice, the engineers in Vietnam, out of necessity, became heavily involved in supply, in that they assisted depots sorting and identifying engineer items, traced and expedited requisitions, and reviewed operations and maintenance and new construction matériel requirements. This was necessary when bulk shipments of literally thousands of tons of engineer matériel were pushed into the country. Control and management of these supplies were overwhelming, and there was a definite need for tighter control.

Only the hard-surfaced highways in Vietnam could be used as main supply routes all year round, and they were constantly mined by the enemy. Until the jungle could be cleared along the sides of the roads, ambushes were frequent. Secondary roads were passable only in the dry season. Consequently, a heavy burden was placed on engineer units in moving construction materials into inland bases. In any future conflict in underdeveloped countries, land-clearing equipment, mine detectors, and road construction equipment should be introduced with the first deployments. There can be no construction until the logistics problems are licked.

CHAPTER X

Lessons and a Legacy

Army base development doctrine before 1965 prescribed that base development plans be prepared at theater level by component representatives. Several base development plans for Southeast Asia were completed. They addressed specific situations with certain assumptions based on U.S. and Vietnamese responses. While the situation which materialized after 1965 was much more extensive and the base development requirements were much greater than those represented in base development plans, Army planning before 1965 should have identified base requirements early in the buildup.

In 1965 there was a Pacific Army plan for South Vietnam, but two significant errors in the operations plan quickly became apparent: the South Vietnamese Army was not as effective as had been anticipated during planning, and U.S. deployments had exceeded the plan.

New buildup plans made between April 1965 and January 1966 set the real scale of base development requirements. Detailed planning was done at the base or installation level with supervisory control at the service level. Control at the service level resulted in competition among construction agencies for limited resources, but management of scarce construction resources improved when the MACV Directorate of Construction was established.

Until June 1965 there were few American engineer troops and only a small contract construction capability in South Vietnam. The buildup had in fact generated a need for far more engineer construction units than existed in the active establishment of all the services. Initially the military construction capability was limited by the decision not to call up the Reserves or National Guard, which contained the bulk of construction units in accordance with Department of Defense policy. Major reliance, therefore, was placed on contractor capability, while the services accelerated programs to increase the number of construction units in the active forces. Based on these considerations and the approved force buildup, a base development plan was devised which consisted of a $1 billion construction program to be accomplished in two years at approximately a $40 million monthly contract placement rate and executed under Navy supervision. Allied engineer troops also performed some construction for their respective forces.

At the beginning of the program there were no set standards except limitations on living space and the general admonition that facilities would be minimum and austere. The basic principle in establishing construction standards was to provide the required facilities for the expected duration of use as cheaply as possible. Theater standards were developed to minimize costs and time. These standards were based on three factors: the mission of the unit for which the facilities were provided, the permanency of units in a given location, and the philosophy of each military service. The problem of establishing standards was complicated by variations in philosophies and the peculiar characteristics of the war.

Although forty-two construction units of battalion strength were deployed to South Vietnam, the requirements for base development were of such magnitude that the contractor force supplied a greater construction capability than the entire military force. This was attributable to the special equipment and personnel that the contractor could mobilize for large projects. Equipment like 30-inch pipeline dredges, 30-ton dump trucks, and 400-ton-per-hour rockcrushers speeded work on big jobs.

Roads were upgraded and surfaced with asphalt paving as a deterrent to clandestine mining and as a solution to subgrade moisture during the monsoon rainfall. Land clearing, 100 meters along each side of the right of way, was a counterinsurgency measure against ambush.

Troop housing was upgraded from tents to tropical wood-frame buildings because of the rapid deterioration of canvas in a tropical environment. The static nature and the long duration of operations made it economical to install better quality more durable utilities and to support services beyond the temporary nature of the designs in Technical Manual 5–302.

Major airfield runways were first constructed at an expeditionary standard and then replaced by concrete runways. Although expedient matting was not durable enough for continuous fighter or heavy transport aircraft operations, it was sufficient for use on the smaller airfields.

Construction in Southeast Asia was funded by a variety of United States sources: the Agency for International Development, Military Assistance Programs, Operations and Maintenance funds, and Military Construction funds. Control was exercised through tight project allocations with most of the work being done by military construction funds allocated by Congress. This type of funding forced extensive preliminary planning and made approved projects somewhat cumbersome to change. For major projects approximately twenty-four months normally elapsed between the development of requirements and final construction. Some of this delay can be attributed to the procurement of materials and some of the administrative requirements that all funds for construction be on hand before the start of construction. Stringent control made changes difficult and did affect over-all operations to some degree because once the sites had been determined for ports and airfields their requirement was subject to change in light of ongoing operations.

Costs for construction in South Vietnam were approximately two and a half times greater than for similar construction in the United States. This is attributable to the 12,000-mile supply line, a premium wage rate for U.S. nationals, the urgency placed on all projects, and the crash nature of the program. As the intensity of hostilities diminishes, many things can be built of local materials by local labor at far less cost.

Contractor costs included an extensive support force (that is, direct labor was 15 percent of the labor force in South Vietnam compared to 60 percent on construction projects in the United States). While tabulated troop construction costs included only the material, the overhead costs were very high because of the combat training needed and the special military support costs.

The construction done in 1965–68 in South Vietnam enabled the United States to deploy and operate a modern 500,000-man military force in an underdeveloped area. The ground combat force of 165,000 men was able to combat an enemy force effectively from an adequate facility base which permitted U.S. and allied forces to concentrate and operate when and where they wished. Most construction was temporary; the more durable construction will become economic assets for South Vietnam. (*Map 12 and Table 5*)

The Army's base development activities in South Vietnam during 1965–68 have been reviewed in a series of assessments: "Observations on the Construction Program Vietnam" by Brigadier General Daniel A. Raymond (June 1967); the Chief of Engineers-sponsored Seeman Board (February 1968); the Joint Chiefs of Staff-sponsored Special Military Construction Study Group (October 1968); and the Office, Secretary of Defense's Joint Logistic Review Board (September 1970). Several major problem areas and corrective actions have been revealed and suggested in these assessments.

The wide disparity of construction standards between the services in Vietnam was particularly evident in cantonment construction. Air Force planners contended that a $100 million base was not a transient facility and wanted more for their money in durable

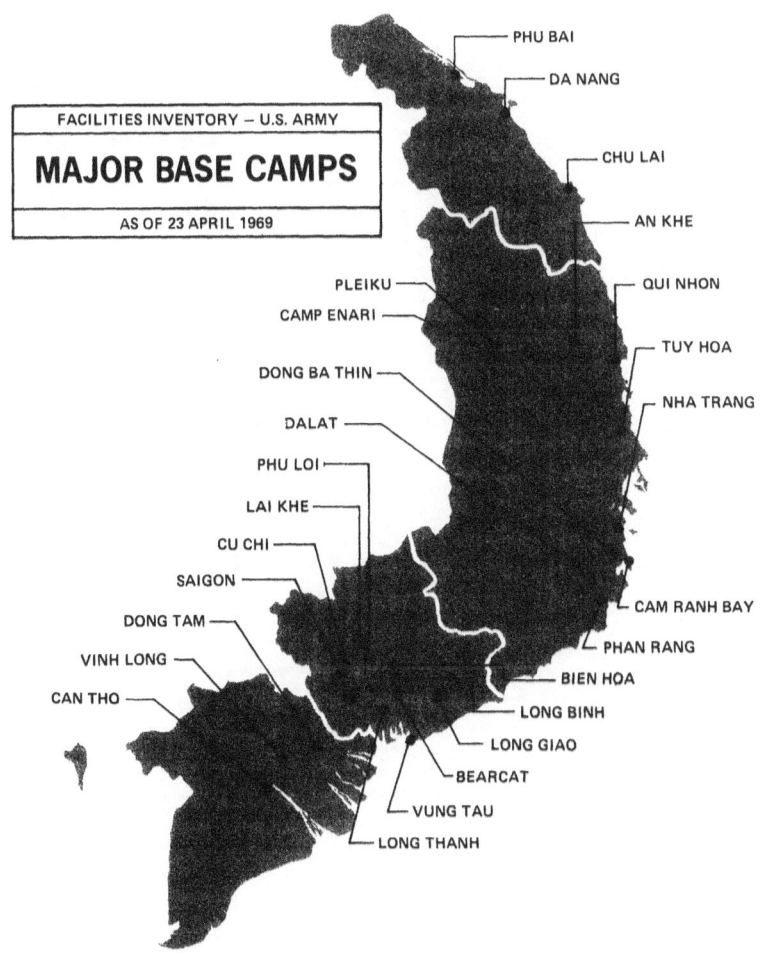

MAP 12

construction. They felt that pilots and electronics technicians lost efficiency when forced to live like combat troops. This caused dissatisfaction between the troops of different services living in the same general area.

The Joint Chiefs of Staff took up the standards of construction problem in November 1969, but left the decision to the President. In June 1970, the Joint Chiefs of Staff Construction Board for Con-

TABLE 5—MAJOR BASE CAMPS

INSTALLATION	CANTONEMENT CAPABILITY			ADMIN. SPACE SQUARE FEET	STORAGE SPACE S			MAINT. SPACE SQUARE FEET
	BASED ON HOUSING		BASED ON W.B.SEWAGE @ 80 GPD/MAN (TOTAL)	BASED ON WATER SUPPLY @ 100 GPD/MAN (TOTAL)		COVERED S.F.	OPEN S.Y.	
	OFFICERS	EM						
PHU BAI	754	5,800	1,000	1,700	93,784	127,983	9,777	48,532
DA NANG	671	4,865	1,150	1,790	106,500	21,634	89,617	114,425
CHU LAI	1,595	10,337	0	4,520	76,615	101,881	56,587	262,949
PLEIKU	611	9,521	0	10,000	119,497	112,669	5,916	100,547
CAMP ENARI	1,023	9,223	0	5,680	300,420	85,600	58,200	218,898
AN KHE	1,950	12,000	0	4,500	259,730	225,492	107,761	188,942
QUI NHON	1,870	20,980	2,065	3,070	519,200	1,050,499	359,242	499,128
TUY HOA	1,002	6,765	750	5,130	116,345	88,438	233,550	92,063
NHA TRANG	438	7,958	5,080	7,340	275,407	306,605	51,840	154,541
DONG BA THIN	563	2,430	0	2,650	38,192	7,600	0	25,220
DALAT	7	579	80	1,000	3,821	17,767	373	1,760
CAM RANH BAY	1,479	17,173	0	10,000	440,900	873,425	622,844	377,795
PHAN RANG	220	4,487	0	720	48,119	48,075	230	11,176
LAI KHE	532	3,706	0	700	72,326	17,038	105,350	26,216
PHU LOI	932	5,721	0	12,500	81,032	36,716	149,055	481,013
CU CHI	1,512	12,616	0	4,500	207,261	125,036	91,560	191,800
BIEN HOA	815	8,407	6,035	22,680	134,597	91,972	3,333	136,353
LONG BINH	5,855	36,987	16,250	25,530	1,085,544	992,655	1,269,901	917,734
BLACK HORSE (LONG GIAO)	307	4,537	0	1,800	79,320	30,302	5,333	6,824
BEARCAT	972	7,615	0	13,200	125,132	60,978	64,207	117,778
MACV—SAIGON—T.S.N.	10,768	23,288	250	14,700	1,143,452	1,453,945	64,813	221,155
SAIGON PORTS	218	1,379	3,875	2,470	163,582	945,499	365,231	61,093
LONG THANH NORTH	189	933	0	5,400	21,808	28,880	27,710	70,050
VUNG TAU	294	8,182	2,625	4,140	136,390	267,757	135,068	331,035
DONG TAM	1,193	10,995	0	6,480	160,210	89,184	11,247	212,266
VINH LONG	365	2,435	188	2,400	11,544	25,951	0	46,582
CAN THO	131	1,915	337	5,120	41,419	32,782	28,050	48,643

tingency Operations made minor modifications to the 1966 standards and suggested the following standards for construction and base development in support of contingency operations:

Field: Cantonments for forces whose activities are such that they may be characterized as essentially transient.

Intermediate: Cantonments for forces subject to move at infrequent intervals. Anticipated duration of occupancy: 24–48 months.

Temporary: Cantonments for forces not expected to move in the foreseeable future.

Experience in Vietnam has shown that a Director of Construction should operate directly under the command of and as part of the staff of the joint commander in the combat area to ensure effective and responsive co-ordination with operations and logistic support. A Director of Construction provides the commander of a joint force with the means of exercising control and direction over construction. The Joint Logistics Review Board suggested that contingency planning set forth the appropriate composition and role of a construction directorate on the staff of the joint field commander.

The board has also made several recommendations pertaining to funding for construction in support of contingency operations, but the funding problem persists pending revision of Department of Defense instructions. While not as detailed as construction programs, base development planning can provide the data necessary to keep construction costs within limits set by funding procedures.

The board further noted that there were no country-to-country agreements or draft agreements in support of contingency plans for Vietnam that could have expedited real-estate acquisition. Also, there were too few trained real estate teams available to meet the needs of the many widely separated bases and operational areas requiring property for the expanding war.

The Joint Chiefs have developed procedural plans to resolve many of our real-estate problems. Base development plans now identify real-estate requirements, existing base rights, and any additional rights that are necessary. Such plans can provide a basis for the start of negotiations for real-estate agreements in areas for which contingency plans have been prepared. The Army has recently organized real estate teams with the capability of deploying into a contingency operation area and augmenting and expediting measures to obtain real estate for American military operations.

Investigations into planning, procurement, and shipping to provide material for construction in Southeast Asia identified several weaknesses in the Engineer Functional Components System. Problems resulted from the differences between standard design and actual requirements and the inability to use the system to initiate procurement and shipping actions. Construction forces and large organizations can achieve considerable savings by planning around local resources and conditions. Designs should be flexible enough to use substitute materials when time or money can be saved. Direct delivery can help maximize savings. In other words, the system should be flexible and allow for special requirements. The inadequacy of base development plans during the Vietnam buildup, for example, has produced new interest in the functional components system. Efforts are under way to update and refine the system, which is now called the Army Facilities Component System, and to make better use of the Army supply system.

As a result of the Special Military Construction Studies Group recommendations in October 1968, the Joint Chiefs established the Joint Staff/Services Construction Board for Contingency Operations. To date, papers have been distributed on suggested standards of construction for cantonments and planning factors for many Department of Defense categories.

Since mid-1968, the Army staff has provided base development planning assistance to the commanders of subordinate Army commands. Eight base plans in support of selected contingency operations have been drafted. Others are being prepared some of which will also serve as joint base development plans. The drafts provide the information and detail required by the Joint Chiefs directive and use automatic data processing to produce the output in hard copy or card decks. Increased use of data processing over the past few years has significantly reduced planning preparation time. Pacific Command Base Development System has recently been improved and simplified to eliminate nonessential data and reduce the work required in developing plans. U.S. Army, Pacific, and the other service component commands assisted in developing these improvements. To reduce further the preparation time and effort of draft base plans, a computer system will soon be available which will perform a major portion of the facilities identification and work calculations.

A proposal is being considered to establish in the Army staff a central planning office for base development. Such an office would support the Army by drafting component and joint base development plans and enhance planning capability by pooling experienced planners with an adequate computer hardware system. The planning office would provide a useful point for liaison with Army and other joint staffs.

The Army Base Development Board (BDB) is sponsored by the

Deputy Chief of Staff for Logistics and was established as a continuing committee on 14 October 1970. Its mission is to evaluate the concepts, management systems, and supporting matériel systems for base development within the Department of the Army. It will determine their adequacy and initiate such measures as necessary to establish staff responsibilities and ensure that Army base development support in future contingency operations is both effective and responsive. This board will maintain the momentum and initiatives started by the joint staff.

Since the Vietnamese will be responsible for the care and maintenance of base facilities and lines of communications, it is important that skilled people be available. For several years U.S. Army engineers have informally given Vietnamese engineer units technical assistance and training to enhance their capability. In October 1968 Major General David S. Parker, then USARV Engineer and Commanding General, Engineer Troops, Vietnam, formally initiated a program of affiliation with Vietnamese engineer units. Through liaison provided by the MACV Engineer Advisor, U.S. engineer units work with their Vietnamese counterparts to complete their projects jointly. Vietnamese engineer troops have been learning the American way of doing things.

In addition to training Vietnamese military personnel, both American military organizations and civilian contractors have hired and trained many Vietnamese civilians to work on construction and maintenance projects. Certainly, the development of a Vietnamese construction capability will probably become the most enduring economic consequence of the base construction program.

In Vietnam, as in other underdeveloped countries, skilled labor has been in short supply. The future progress of these nations depends to a marked degree on the presence of an adequate labor force. At the beginning of the American buildup in 1965, nearly three-quarters of the Vietnamese labor force was engaged in agriculture and related occupations. There was a severe shortage of skilled workers. While some were skilled in basic carpentry, masonry, sheet-metal handling, and electrical work, few were familiar with modern construction methods or equipment, and many had been inducted into the armed forces.

This situation was caused in part by an educational philosophy which honors the diploma more than the skills it is supposed to represent. In Vietnam manually skilled workers have been denied the status and earnings commensurate with the value of their skills to society. As taught in the Vietnamese schools, manual and vocational training prepare the student for semiprofessional occupations rather than for the actual building trades.

Corporal Mung, *103d Engr. Bn., ARVN*, directs his construction crew in pile driving for a new bridge.

The arrival of American military and contractor organizations created an overwhelming demand for construction workers. There not being enough in Vietnam, some workers were recruited from America and from the Philippine Islands, Taiwan, and Korea. So acute was the shortage of trained workers that contractors had to hire unskilled local nationals and show them what tools to use and how to use them.

In the earliest stages of wartime vocational training, workers received on-the-job training to satisfy the immediate needs of a particular employer. The unskilled were assigned as helpers to pick up whatever they could by observation and practice. Gradually, as they proved they could handle the equipment, they were left more and more on their own. Manual training later advanced from on-the-job training to formal programs with full-time "foremen-operators" as instructors. Trainees then learned how to operate different machines and fully to understand equipment capabilities.

At its peak in July 1966, RMK–BRJ employed some 50,000 Vietnamese at fifty locations. Because of the labor turnover caused by the draft or by the reluctance of the Vietnamese to relocate on jobs farther from their homes, RMK by 1970 had cumulatively hired more than 200,000 persons. Among those trained at contractor run schools were accountants, clerk-typists, engineer-draftsmen, auto mechanics and painters, drivers, electricians, machinists, heavy-equipment operators, refrigeration and air-conditioning maintenance men, and welders. Besides acquiring technical skills, all students also studied English.

Between 1965 and 1970 Pacific Architects and Engineers trained some 23,000 Vietnamese in various facets of facilities engineering—in the operation and maintenance of boiler plants, water plants, kitchen equipment, generators, and refrigeration and air-conditioning equipment—as well as firefighters, engineer-draftsmen, auto mechanics, electricians, heavy-equipment operators, and stock clerks. In 1966 PA&E established a training department in Saigon for both formal and on-the-job training. One of its most successful projects has been the training of women to work as welders, carpenters, generator operators, crane operators, and vehicle operators.

In addition, engineer units of the U.S. Army, Navy, and Air Force have trained thousands of other Vietnamese civilians. During October 1967 the U.S. Army Engineer Command, Vietnam, employed over 8,500 Vietnamese, many of whom acquired new skills and insights through this experience.

As the Joint Development Group has pointed out, the improved skill base will strengthen Vietnam's postwar economy. Those ex-servicemen and civilians who have worked in war-related construction will be able to transfer readily to peacetime reconstruction. It is expected that most will find suitable employment in private and public sectors. Civil projects will include programs for the repair and maintenance of highways, bridges, and railroads, and projects for water control, irrigation, and land reclamation needed

STUDENT VOLUNTEERS *help construct a dormitory for war orphans at the Buddhist Institute, Saigon.*

for agricultural expansion. Thus these people will form a base of skilled labor in postwar Vietnam and will make a significant contribution to the development of their homeland.

General Westmoreland had established a priority system for the turnover of U.S. developed property. Although all facilities and bases will be given to the Vietnamese as part of the Vietnamization process, a claim system allows other U.S. forces to have a last chance at property being disposed of. The order runs thus: U.S. forces, Vietnamese armed forces, U.S. forces outside Vietnam, and other U.S. agencies. Between 11 September 1969 and 15 September 1970, thirty-nine installations were transferred to the Vietnamese Army. Total acquisition cost of these facilities was $43,428,000. Among the more valuable were 4 divisional bases, costing $23,950,000; 2 minor ports, costing $7,544,000; 2 compounds, costing $2,556,000; and 2 cantonments, costing $2,547,000.

In some respects the task of building a military base is comparable to that of building a town. Perhaps the major difference is that bases are planned to serve specific ends, while towns are usually unplanned and grow on the basis of expediency rather than purpose. Typical military bases contain cantonments, storage facilities, roads, electric power plants, communications centers, water supply and sewage systems, and provisions for security. Bases may also include airfields, ports, and fuel storage and distribution facilities. We can look back now to some of the outstanding base facilities and related engineering left to our Vietnamese allies.

Initially the port of Saigon provided the only unloading facilities for oceangoing vessels. Its six deep-draft berths were altogether inadequate for handling regular commercial shipping and the hundreds of ships bringing military cargo from America. The result was an enlarging of port facilities fivefold.

In the spring of 1965 Army engineer troops moved to Cam Ranh Bay, an excellent natural but a wholly undeveloped harbor. There they installed a DeLong pier and a causeway pier that enabled four ships to unload simultaneously. Six more berths were subsequently constructed in this harbor.

To handle military cargo in the Saigon area, the Newport port facilities were constructed by RMK–BRJ on what had been rice-paddy land two miles north of Saigon. *(Map 13)* As silt from the river bottom was unsuitable for fill, great quantities of rock and sand were brought in by barge and truck. Newport can accommodate simultaneously 4 oceangoing vessels, 4 shallow-draft landing craft, and 7 barges. The cost was nearly $25 million.

Deepwater berths and appurtenant coastal facilities have also been constructed at Da Nang, Qui Nhon, Vung Tau, and Vung Ro.

Vietnam has been the scene of one of the world's largest dredging operations. Since 1966, fourteen or more dredges have been doing harbor and land-fill work. They have cleared and deepened harbors, rivers, and canals; stockpiled sand for road and base camp construction; and reclaimed land for military, industrial, and housing sites. Without continuing dredging operations the accumulation of silt will, however, close the harbors and inland waterways to navigation.

Eight airfields designed to accommodate large jet aircraft were constructed at Da Nang, Chu Lai, Phu Cat, Tuy Hoa, Cam Ranh Bay, Phan Rang, Bien Hoa, and Tan Son Nhut. These are huge installations with 10,000-foot runways and the whole range of appurtenant facilities, including administrative buildings, hospitals, hangars, repair shops, warehouses, barracks, and mess halls. In November 1967, of ninety other airfields using expedient surfacing materials, eleven were operational for jets and sixty-two for C–130 medium cargo aircraft.

A massive well-drilling program has accompanied the buildup of American forces in Vietnam. Although USAID had sponsored well-drilling in Vietnam since 1957, MACV had to develop its own water supply for its bases. Major work was done under contract to the Navy's OICC. Between July 1966 and September 1967, con-

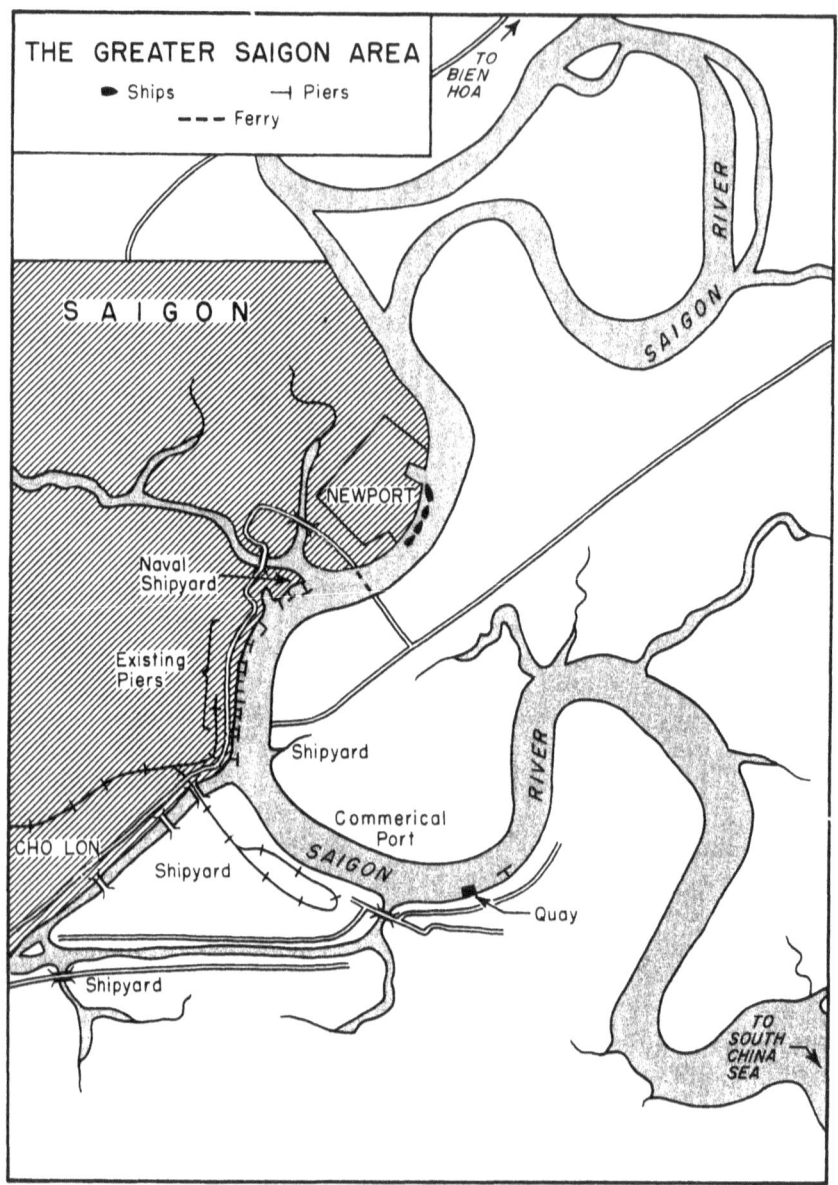

MAP 13

tractors drilled 233 successful wells and 48 test holes at twenty-five sites. These wells had an average depth of 170 feet and an average test yield of 96 gallons per minute. Additional wells have been drilled by Engineer Well Drilling detachments. As of 1 December 1967, 100 wells had been developed and 14 more were under way.

Besides wells now in production, the records of the well-drilling program will be valuable to geologists and engineers charged in peacetime with the responsibility for developing Vietnam's water resources.

"Pentagon East," as the MACV command post has been called, was constructed near Tan Son Nhut Airport. Its network of two-story prefabricated buildings provides air-conditioned working space for 4,000 men. In addition to cantonments and utilities, it includes mortar shelters, security fences, and guard towers. The headquarters complex for USARV was constructed at Long Binh, sixteen miles from Saigon. It occupies twenty-five square miles and houses 50,000 soldiers at a cost of more than $100 million.

A mere cataloging of works performed by engineer troops would more than fill the pages of this study. Among the major projects under construction by engineer troops at the beginning of 1968—the last year of major construction—were fifteen cantonments large enough to accommodate from 4,000 to more than 17,000 men.

The Road Restoration Program was the largest project of its kind ever undertaken by the U.S. military in a foreign country. It was started under USAID totally and transferred to MACV control in September of 1968. Priorities had been jointly established by military and civil authorities. The goal was to construct and upgrade 4,300 kilometers of national and interprovincial highways, replacing obsolete French standards with those of American highway engineers. When completed the system of two-lane all-weather roads will pass through the delta, Saigon, northward along the coast, and into the Central Highlands. Standard bridge designs and standard highway and bridge marking and numbering procedures have been adopted.

This vast highway restoration project will strengthen the unity and the economy of Vietnam. Lacking the air mobility of USARV, the Vietnamese will utilize the roads to deploy swiftly toward Communist-menaced communities. The roads will end the isolation of rural areas and open them to trade.

Since 1967 an independent research agency, the Joint Development Group, has been studying the economic prospects of postwar Vietnam. Many of the facilities discussed in this chapter have also been examined by the group from a economic point of view. The group notes that the ports, airfields, highways, and railroads built or repaired under military auspices will amply satisfy the needs of an expanding national development.

The new and improved seaports should greatly improve coastal and international shipping and travel. The airfields have already made Vietnam an important part of the international air network.

Newly Trained Army Engineers *return to the task of nation building.*

The highway development program is multiplying contacts between villagers and townspeople and enables both to transport goods and commodities farther, faster, cheaper, and safer. Peasants are rebuilding homes and reworking fields that they had abandoned under

Communist pressure before the roads were built. New trading centers accompany the restoration of the roads.

Clean, potable water should reduce the incidence of infectious debilitating diseases. Improved water supply should lower the rates in infant mortality and adult chronic illness.

When peace comes, new uses will be found for the military building complexes. Some of the buildings may be converted into schools, housing, factories, warehouses, shops, or offices.

The ravages of rot, jungle, and weather have left only memories of the once-mighty World War II bases of the South Pacific. The pessimist may predict that such will be the fate of the bases in Vietnam. The future, however, is likely to prove that the Vietnamese are too resourceful not to find applications for many of the facilities left behind to them.

Glossary

ABFC	Advanced Base Functional Components (System). A complete system developed by the Navy containing prefabricated structures, equipment, and packaging for advanced base building.
Aggregate	Crushed rock used with cement to form concrete.
AID	Agency for International Development, which provides resources for underdeveloped nations through the State Department.
Alluvial soil	Consists largely of deposits left by flowing waters.
AM–2	Aluminum matting used to construct runways. It is designed to be portable and rapidly emplaced.
Annam	The original name of the country which is now the Republic of Vietnam.
Backhoe	An excavating machine in which a bucket is rigidly attached to a hinged boom and is drawn toward the machine in digging.
Bailey panel bridge	A pre-engineered semiportable tactical bridge of World War II vintage. Having its structural members above the roadway, the Bailey is a continuous truss bridge joined beneath by flat panel transoms.
BARC	Barge, amphibious, resupply, cargo. A true amphibian duplex-drive transporter. The largest LARC with a 40-ton capacity.
BEEF teams	Base emergency engineering force teams. Small Air Force detachments for construction of critical facilities.
Bladder system	An inflatable fuel container system.

Borrow	Earth used in making fill for construction projects.
C–7 Caribou	Twin-engine utility aircraft designed for short landings and takeoffs from unprepared landing areas.
CENCOM	Central Highways and Waterways Committee of the government of Vietnam.
CINCPAC	Commander in Chief, Pacific. Traditionally a naval Commander, CINCPAC controls all service forces in the Pacific area and reports directly to the Joint Chiefs of Staff.
CINCPACAF	Commander in Chief, Pacific Air Forces, who reports directly to CINCPAC.
CINCPACFLT	Commander in Chief, Pacific Fleet. The commander for ships afloat; he reports to CINCPAC.
CINCUSARPAC	Commander in Chief, U.S. Army, Pacific. He is responsible to CINCPAC.
COMUSMACV	Commander, U.S. Military Assistance Command, Vietnam.
Chlorinator	A device for combining chlorine with water for sterilization.
Clam	Clamshell. A hinged-door bucket for a crane. Also known as a grab bucket.
Compacted	Soil compressed by rolling to reduce surface volume in preparation for construction.
CONEX	A reusable metal shipping container designed for worldwide movement of military equipment through the cargo transporter service.
Creosoted timbers	Piles and other timbers treated with wood-tar distillate as a preservative.
CTZ	Corps tactical zone. American military divisions of Vietnam in four areas.
DGOH	Directorate General of Highways. An office of the government of Vietnam.

GLOSSARY

Democratic Republic of Vietnam	Communist North Vietnam.
Depth of refusal	Depth at which terminal resistance is met in driving operations.
Direct support maintenance	Maintenance performed by units not attached to the using unit. A category of maintenance limited to repair of end items or unserviceable assemblies on a return to user basis. Formerly third echelon.
DMZ	The Demilitarized Zone. A six-mile strip which roughly parallels the Song Ben Hoi separating North from South Vietnam.
DSA	Defense Supply Agency. The purchasing agent for common supply items in the Department of Defense.
Erdlator	A clarifier used in water purification units in conjunction with diatomite earth filters.
Engineer Service, Army	A World War II and Korean building appropriation fund.
Foreshore area	That area between high- and low-water marks.
FFV	Field Force, Vietnam. A flexible corps level headquarters organization designed to control Army units of all sizes. Became I Field Force August 1966.
FWMAF	Free World Military Assistance Forces. Included at times: Australian battalions, Korean divisions, New Zealand company-sized units, Philippine civic action group, and Thai regiments.
Hopper dredge	A dredge using hydraulic suction pipes to excavate bottom material into internal hoppers as opposed to separate barges. This dredge can carry its own waste to a dumping area. Unlike other plants, this one is self-propelled and fully seaworthy.
Horizontal construction	Roads, canals, etc. as opposed to vertical construction—dwellings, sheds, etc.

Hue	Former capital of Annamese Empire. Ancient city considered cultural center for Vietnam. Scene of bitter street fighting in 1968 *Tet* offensive.
GAME WARDEN	A code name for naval river patrol operations.
ICC	International Control Commission established by 1954 Geneva Convention consisting of representatives from Canada, India, and Poland.
ICTZ	I Corps Tactical Zone. The northernmost provinces in South Vietnam.
IFFORCEV	I Field Force, Vietnam.
JCS	Joint Chiefs of Staff. Includes Chief of Staff, Army; Chief of Staff, Air Force; Chief of Naval Operations; Commandant of the Marine Corps; and the chairman. This is a planning and advisory staff without command authority.
JGS	Joint General Staff. Vietnamese equivalent of our JCS.
JLRB	Joint Logistics Review Board. Investigative body which met during 1969 to formulate recommendations on logistics.
Keppel Yards	Singapore shipyard contracted for marine repairs.
LARC	Amphibian lighter. Duplex-drive amphibian descendant of World War II DUKW. V series has 5-ton capacity, XV series 15 tons. Also fitted for recovery.
Laterite	A red ferruginous soil containing iron and alumina.
LCM	Landing craft, mechanized.
LCU	Landing craft, utility.
LOC	Lines of Communications.
LSD	Landing ship, dock. Ship having a cargo deck which carries amphibian transporters; to launch, the cargo deck is flooded and the stern opens to the sea.

GLOSSARY

LZ	Landing zone.
MACV	Military Assistance Command, Vietnam. Established in February 1962 at Saigon from the former Military Assistance Advisory Group.
MAF	III (Third) Marine Amphibious Force. USMC headquarters formed in May 1965 from the former 9th Marine Expeditionary Brigade to control elements of 1st, 3d, 5th Marine Divisions and 1st Marine Air Wing.
MAP	Military Assistance Program controls sales of American military equipment worldwide.
Marine wood borers	Organisms which feed on wood structures at and below water level and cause rapid structural decay.
Market Time	Code name for naval coastal patrol operations.
MCA	Military Construction, Army. An appropriation specifically for new construction.
MCB	Naval mobile construction battalions. "Seabees."
MILCON	Military Construction or construction funded by MCA funds.
MSR	Main supply route.
NAVFORV	Naval Forces, Vietnam. All naval forces afloat and ashore in Vietnam.
NSA	Naval Support Activity. Consists of shore facilities to support operations afloat and land-based naval aircraft.
OMA	Operations and Maintenance, Army, funds. Appropriations for repair and maintenance of existing facilities.
PA&E	Pacific Architects and Engineers.
PACAF	Pacific Air Forces. All Air Force units in Pacific area including 5th Air Force in Korea, 7th Air Force in Vietnam, etc.
PACOM	Pacific Command. Unified command of CINCPAC, CINCPACAF, CINCUSARPAC and commanded by CINCPAC.

Pipeline cutter-head dredge	A dredge in which a steel basket-shaped cutterhead surrounds the suction pipe intake. Pipelines carry the bottom material ashore or overboard.
Plastic membrane seal	Rolled sheets of thin flexible plastic used to cover soil and prevent erosion.
POL	Petroleum, oil, and lubricants.
Potable	Suitable, safe, or ready for drinking.
Prime BEEF teams	Air Force base emergency engineer forces.
Red Ball	A designation for specially expedited repair parts and supplies having very high priority.
Red Horse	Air Force heavy repair squadron.
Riprap	Large crushed and random-sized rock used in construction without cement.
RMK–BRJ	Contracting combine of Raymond, Morrison-Knudson, Brown and Root, and J. A. Jones.
ROK	Republic of Korea.
SATS	Short airfield for tactical support. Portable runways and facilities for service, landings, and takeoffs. Makes use of AM–2 panels and mobile command control equipment.
Sheet piles	Sheet steel formed for pile driving and designed to interlock forming retaining walls.
T–2 Tanker	An electrical power ship. Tankers withdrawn from Maritime Reserve Fleet and converted to electrical power barges by Vinnell Corp. T–2 designates Maritime Commission class size.
Tank farm	Petroleum storage area.
Turnkey	A contract that makes the contractor responsible for all phases of the work, to include administrative and logistical support from design through completion of construction.
USAECAV	U.S. Army Engineer Construction Agency, Vietnam.

GLOSSARY

USARYIS	U.S. Army, Ryukyu Islands.
USAMC	U.S. Army Materiel Command.
USAPAV	U.S. Army Procurement Agency, Vietnam. Responsible for administering of all civilian contracts and local outside purchases.
USARPAC	U.S. Army, Pacific.
USARV	U.S. Army, Vietnam. A headquarters primarily responsible for logistics, administration, and support for MACV.

Index

ADAMS huts: 88
Administrative facilities construction: 77
Advanced Base Functional Component System, U.S. Navy: 47, 127
Advisers, U.S.: 6, 14, 139
Agreement for Mutual Defense Assistance in Indochina: 29
Air bases: 38–40, 44, 57, 60–64
Air conditioning: 44, 79–80, 145
Air Force, Seventh: 26, 30
Air Vietnam: 7
Airborne Brigade, 173d: 19–20
Airborne Division, 101st: 74
Aircraft
  C-123: 69
  C-130: 19, 68–69, 143
  CV-2: 63
  protective structures: 65–68
Airfields, construction and repair: 63–64, 69, 133, 143, 145
Airports: 7
Aluminum, in construction: 88
Ambushes: 131
American Association of State Highway Officials: 100
Ammunition supply: 85–86
An Khe: 68, 72, 75, 126
Annam, kingdom of: 5–6
Annamite Mountains (Cordillera): 3
Antarctica: 17
Assistant Chief of Staff for Logistics, MACV: 17
Australia and Australian forces: 73, 109, 113

Backhoes: 106
Bailey bridge: 73
Bangkok: 17
Barges
  in POL supply: 125
  quartering on: 73
Base Development Branch, J-4: 17
Base Emergency Engineering Forces, U.S. Air Force: 17, 27, 65, 90

Base facilities. *See also* Bases; Construction, general.
  construction and expansion: 68–70
  construction standards: 46
  operation: 40
  sites, acquisition: 53
  troop support capacity: 68–69
Bases
  construction, extent of: 143–45
  construction programs: 72–74, 145
  construction standards: 45–46, 74, 133, 135–37
  cost per man: 74
  development doctrine and plans: 132–33, 138–39
  hotel concept: 75
  number of units built: 73
  physical arrangement: 68
  transfer to Republic of Vietnam: 142, 147
  USARV construction study: 73–75
Beach grading: 56–57
Bien Hoa: 7, 19–20, 38, 69, 111, 126, 143
Binh Dinh: 9
Binh Tuy: 9
Bladders, fuel storage: 129
Boundaries, national: 3
Bradley, Major General William T.: 30
Bridges
  construction and repair: 73, 99–100, 145
  local types: 9
  number needed and built: 106, 111
  types planned: 106–107
Brown & Root. *See* RMK–BRJ.
BUSH (Buy U.S. Here) Program: 87

Ca Mau Peninsula: 5
Caltex: 124
Cam Ranh Bay: 19–21, 38, 50–52, 54–57, 59, 61, 68–69, 71–72, 75, 77, 79–80, 84, 86, 91–92, 110, 117, 126, 143
Cam Ranh Support Command: 92
Cambodia: 9, 29

Can Tho: 30, 38, 69, 125-26
Canals: 5
Cantonments. *See* Bases; Housing.
Cavalry Division, 1st: 19
Cement mixers: 106-107
Central Highlands: 5, 9, 106, 145
Central Highways and Waterways Coordination Committee: 100
Central Real Estate Office: 30-31
Che Reo: 68
Chief of Engineers, Republic of Vietnam Armed Forces: 18
Chief of Engineers, U.S. Army: 35, 97, 134
China: 5-6, 113
Cho Gao (dredge): 53
Chu Lai: 32, 38, 52, 61-63, 68, 126, 143
Cities, movement from: 77
Civil Operations and Rural Development Support (CORDS) : 28
Climate: 3
Coastline: 3
Cogido: 59
Cold storage. *See* Refrigeration facilities.
Colonization: 6
Commander, Naval Forces, Vietnam: 25, 30
Commander, Service Forces, Pacific: 126
Commander in Chief, Pacific (CINCPAC). *See* Felt, Admiral Harry D.; Pacific Command; Sharp, Admiral U. S. Grant.
Commander in Chief, Pacific Fleet: 126
Commerce, Republic of Vietnam: 6-7
Communications system
 construction program: 77-78
 operation: 91
Computer equipment: 114-15, 138
Congress: 43, 46, 48-49
Construction, general. *See also by type.*
 agencies engaged: 27-28, 132-33
 agreements on: 137
 by Air Force: 26-27
 appropriations, 1965-69: 49
 assessments of: 134
 austerity in: 41-42, 47, 133
 benefits to South Vietnam: 145-47
 components system: 47
 control and jurisdiction of: 16-17, 19, 21-24, 41, 43, 133
 costs: 18, 46, 134
 directives on: 43

Construction, general—Continued
 elements required: 40-41
 extent of: 134, 145
 funds, authorization: 47-49, 133-34, 137
 materials, acquiring: 137-38
 monitoring. *See* control and jurisdiction of, *above.*
 by Navy: 25-27, 47, 52
 plans, development of: 40, 115-16
 prefabricated techniques: 87-88, 145
 priorities, establishing: 37, 41
 reprograming: 49
 standards: 43-47, 96, 134-38
Construction Board for Contingency Operations: 135-37
Construction machinery: 103-104, 120-22, 124, 133
Construction materials: 115-20, 124
Construction Materials-Special Handling: 118
Contractors, civilian: 16-17, 25-27 42-43, 78, 83-84, 89-96, 122, 124, 133
Contracts, administration of: 92-93
Coral, use in construction: 56-57
Corps of Engineers: 17
Corps Tactical Zones
 I: 9, 19, 24-25, 30, 38, 52, 68-69, 90-91, 93, 117, 129
 II: 9, 19, 24-25, 30, 38-40, 68, 117, 126
 III: 9, 20, 24-25, 30, 69, 102, 117, 126
 IV: 9, 20, 24-25, 30, 53, 69, 102, 117, 126
Cu Chi: 73
Cube piers: 57-58
Cultural history: 5-6
Culverts, construction and repair: 106
Curb extruders: 106

Da Nang: 7, 9, 19, 38, 47, 50, 52, 54, 59-60, 68-69, 72, 86-88, 91, 110, 125-26, 128-29, 143
Da Nang Bay: 125
Davison (dredge): 52
Deadline rate: 121-22
Defense, Department of: 16-17, 25, 49. *See also* McNamara, Robert S.
Defense Fuel Supply Center: 126
DeLong Corporation: 27
DeLong pier: 54-55, 57, 59, 143
Delta region: 5, 9, 11, 73, 107, 145
Demilitarized Zone (DMZ): 3, 126
Depots. *See* Base facilities; Bases.

INDEX

Deputy Assistant Secretary of Defense (Installations and Housing): 43
Deputy Assistant Secretary of Defense (Properties and Installations): 17
Deputy Chief of Staff for Logistics: 139
Deputy J-4 for Engineering, USMACV: 18
Deputy Officer in Charge of Construction, Southeast Asia: 45
Deputy Secretary of Defense. *See* Vance, Cyrus R.
Di An: 73
Director General of Highways, Republic of Vietnam: 22, 99–100
Directorate of the Army MAP Logistics: 18
Directorate of Construction, USMACV: 100–101
  activation: 18, 30, 132
  authority: 19
  command and staff structure: 14–18, 21–23
  land acquisition by: 29–30
  mission: 18–19, 23
  staff function: 137
Directorate of Water Supply, Republic of Vietnam: 11
Diseases, endemic: 11, 97
Dispensaries, construction standards: 45
District engineer offices: 92
Dong Ba Thin: 73
Dong Ha: 108
Dong Na Delta: 11
Dong Nai River: 59
Dong Tam: 53, 73
Dredging operations: 52–54, 73, 80, 143
Dump trucks: 105
Dunn, Major General Carroll H.: 18
Dust, control and effect of: 11–12, 65

Earth compactors: 105
Economy, local: 6–7, 60, 145
Eiffel bridge: 73
Eisenhower, Dwight D.: 6
Electric plants
  construction program: 78–83
  construction standards: 45
  ships' use as: 78–80
Electric power, demands for: 44–45, 47
Engineer Battalions
  20th: 21
  39th: 21

Engineer Battalions—Continued
  62d: 62
  70th: 21
  84th: 20, 57
  864th: 20
Engineer Brigades
  18th: 21, 23–24, 51, 59, 103
  20th: 24, 103
Engineer Companies
  173d: 20
  497th: 51, 55–58
  572d: 21
Engineer Detachments
  64th: 29
  536th: 59
Engineer Division, J-4, USMACV: 18
Engineer Functional Components System: 47, 116, 118, 137–38
Engineer Groups
  35th: 20
  159th: 20
  937th: 21, 59
Engineer Service, Army: 47–48
Engineer units
  arrivals and departures: 17, 20–21, 107
  combat role: 102
  supply role: 131
  training of Republic of Vietnam Armed Forces: 139
  troop strength, periodic: 21, 26–27, 133
Engineering for facilities
  command structure: 92
  defined: 89–90
  extent of: 96
  lessons learned: 98
  regulations, application of: 94
  work force required: 98
Esso: 124
Euclid dump trucks: 105
Exports, South Vietnam: 6–7

Farmland: 3–5
Felt, Admiral Harry D.: 13, 15, 125
Field Force, II: 20, 73
Fill operations: 52–53, 58, 99, 143
Fire preventing and fighting: 96–97
Fleet Marine Force, Pacific: 27
Foremost Dairy: 72
Fort Belvoir, Virginia: 51
Fort Bragg, North Carolina: 20
Fort Hood, Texas: 20
Fort Mason, California: 123

France: 6, 29
Fuel supply. *See* POL supplies.

GAME WARDEN: 69
Garrett Air Research Company: 76
Generators, electrical: 78–79, 83
Geneva Accords (1954): 3, 6, 108
Go Vap: 125
Graves, relocating: 35
Guantánamo Bay: 17
Gutter systems: 106

Han dynasty: 5
Hanoi: 9
Harbor Clearance Unit One, U.S. Navy: 54
Harkins, General Paul D.: 13–14
Hawaii: 78
Headquarters Support Activity, Saigon, U.S. Navy: 26, 91, 114
Heat, effect of: 12
Heiser, Major General Joseph M., Jr.: 119
Helicopters: 65
Heliports: 64–65
Highways. *See* National Route 1, 13, and 14; Roads.
Hospital facilities
   construction program: 75–77
   construction standards: 47
Housing
   construction standards: 45–46
   improving: 72, 133
Hue: 7, 38, 62–63, 68, 99, 110
Hyde (dredge): 52
Hydrant fueling systems: 125

Ice plants: 72
Imports, South Vietnam: 7
Infantry Brigades
   1st, 101st Airborne Division: 19
   2d, 1st Infantry Division: 19
   3d, 25th Infantry Division: 20
Infantry Divisions
   1st: 19, 73
   9th: 73
Inflating, controlling: 59
Interior Ministerial Real Estate Committee, Republic of Vietnam: 29, 31, 52
Inventory control: 115, 117–18
Inventory Control Center, 14th: 114–15, 118

Jamaica Bay (dredge): 53
Japan: 6, 16–17, 78
Jetties, construction and repair: 57
Johnson, Lyndon B.: 15, 19, 42
Joint Chiefs of Staff: 62–63, 127, 134–38
Joint Development Group: 141, 145
Joint General Staff, Republic of Vietnam: 16, 30, 77, 100
Joint Logistics Review Board: 134, 137
Joint Staff/Services Construction Board for Contingency Operations: 138
Joint United States Public Affairs Office (JUSPAO): 28
Jones, J. A. (contractor). *See* RMK–BRJ.

Kennedy, John F.: 6
Kennedy, Colonel Kenneth W.: 18
Keppel Yards: 54
Kidde (Walter) Constructors: 27
Kontum City: 9, 68
Kublai Khan: 6

Labor force, civilian: 90–91, 107, 134, 139, 141
Lai Khe: 73
Lam Dong: 9
Land acquisition. *See* Real estate.
Land-clearing operations: 32, 112, 131, 133
Landing craft, mechanized (LCM): 58
Landing craft, utility (LCU): 58
Landing ship, tank (LST): 55–56, 59, 68–69
Laos: 9, 16, 29
Latrines: 84
Lien Chieu: 125, 130–31
Loc Ninh: 108
Logistical Command, 1st: 14–15, 19, 21, 23, 30–31, 51, 92, 114, 117–19, 122
Logistical operations: 17, 40, 93. *See also* Supply operations.
   combat support: 113
   deficiencies in: 113–15
   manuals as guides: 115–16
   planning, need for: 131
   reorganization: 114–15
   support of: 113–14
Logistics Control Office, Pacific: 123

INDEX

Long Binh: 31, 59, 72–73, 77, 79–80, 84, 88, 102–103, 111, 113, 117, 126, 145
Long Thanh: 73
Lubricants. *See* POL supplies.

McNamara, Robert S.: 18–19, 41, 43, 48–49, 62. *See also* Defense, Department of.
Maintenance and repair: 96, 114, 121–22
Manpower, skilled, lack of and training: 42, 78, 89, 91, 94, 98, 121, 131, 137, 139–42
Marble Mountain: 129
Marine Amphibious Force, III: 25
Marine Director of Public Works, Republic of Vietnam: 100
Marine Divisions, 1st and 3d: 68
Marine Regiment, 4th: 61
Maritime Reserve Fleet: 78
MARKET TIME: 68–69
Matting, aluminum: 61, 63–65, 67
Meadowgold Dairies: 72
Mechanics. *See* Manpower.
Medical supply: 114
Medical unit, self-contained, transportable (MUST): 75–77
Mediterranean theater: 17
Mekong Delta. *See* Delta region.
Mekong River: 5, 7
Mess halls, construction: 45
Military Assistance Advisory Group (MAAG): 13–14
Military Assistance Program: 6, 17, 29, 133
Military Rail Security Forces, Republic of Vietnam: 109
Military zones: 9. *See also* Corps Tactical Zones.
Milk plants: 72
Mineral resources: 7
Ministry of Public Works, Communications and Transportation, Republic of Vietnam: 18, 23
Mobile Construction Battalion Ten, U.S. Navy: 61
Modular buildings: 88
Modular storage system: 87
Moisture, effect of: 12
Monsoons: 3, 12, 52, 65
MOOSE: 77
Morrison–Knudsen. *See* RMK–BRJ.

My Tho: 73
My Tho River: 53–54

Nai Hon: 125
National Highway Training School, Republic of Vietnam: 100
National Railway System, Republic of Vietnam: 19
National Route 1: 9, 99, 109
National Route 13: 9
National Route 14: 9
Naval Construction Regiment, 30th: 27
Naval Facilities Engineering Command: 17, 27
Near East theater: 17
New Jersey (dredge): 53–54
New Zealand: 113
Newport: 59, 69, 111, 114, 143
Nguyen family: 6
Nha Be: 124–25, 130–31
Nha Trang: 7, 20, 30, 38, 50, 52, 56, 69, 73, 77, 79–80, 110, 126
Ninh Hoa: 69, 110
Nitze, Paul H.: 62
Noble, Brigadier General Charles C.: 43
Nui Sap Quarry: 100

Oil supplies. *See* POL supplies.
Okinawa: 17, 50, 55
Operations and maintenance funds: 47–48, 117–19, 133

Pacific Architects and Engineers, Inc.: 26–27, 31, 72, 79, 89–97, 141
Pacific Command: 13, 15–17, 25, 40, 77–78, 138. *See also* Felt, Admiral Harry D.; Sharp, Admiral U. S. Grant.
Pacific Fleet: 25
Page Communications Engineers: 78
Palmer, Lieutenant General Bruce, Jr.: 74–75
Parker, Major General David S.: 139
Paving program: 105–106
Pentalateral Agreement for Free World Military Assistance Forces: 29
Perkins, Bert: 25
Pest control and eradication: 97–98
Petroleum supplies. *See* POL supplies.
Phan Rang: 38, 52, 62, 69, 72, 74, 110, 126, 143
Phan Thiet: 99, 126
Philco-Ford: 27, 90–91, 93

Philippines: 16, 78, 113, 140
Phu Bai: 52
Phu Cat: 38, 68, 109–10, 143
Piers, construction and repair: 38, 54–55, 57–59, 143
Pipelines: 59, 125–26, 129–30
Plain of Reeds: 5
Pleiku City: 20, 68, 71, 126
Ploger, Brigadier General Robert R.: 21
POL supplies: 124–31
Political structure, South Vietnam: 6–7, 9
Population, South Vietnam: 5, 7
Ports
  construction: 38, 51–53, 56–60
  development and expansion: 51, 114, 143, 145
  lack of: 7, 37–38, 50
  sites, acquiring: 52–53
Post exchanges: 44

Quang Duc: 9
Qui Nhon: 21, 30, 38, 50, 52, 54–55, 57–59, 68–69, 72–73, 75, 77, 79–80, 86, 91–93, 110, 117, 125–26, 131, 143
Qui Nhon Support Command: 71, 92

Railways
  benefits to South Vietnam from: 109–11
  capacity and mileage: 109–12
  construction and repair: 108–11
  damage, typhoon and enemy: 109
  local nets: 7–9, 37, 108
  rolling stock procurement: 109
  U.S. grants for: 109
Rainfall: 3, 11–12, 83
Raymond, Brigadier General Daniel A.: 18, 134
Raymond International. *See* RMK–BRJ.
Real estate
  agreements on: 29, 81–83, 86, 137
  claims for: 32, 142
  costs of leasing: 31–32
  jurisdiction over acquiring: 30
  leasing procedures: 30–34
  lessons from leasing: 35–36
  managing: 33–34
  number of leases: 33
  property accountability: 35
  rentals, co-ordinating: 35
Reconnaissance, aerial: 64

Red Ball Express: 122–23
Red Horse squadrons, U.S. Air Force: 17, 27, 90
Red River: 5
Refrigeration facilities: 44, 71–72
Repair parts: 120–22
Repairs. *See* Maintenance and repair.
Republic of Korea: 16–17, 19, 68, 73, 78, 103, 140
Republic of Vietnam Armed Forces (RVNAF): 113, 126, 132, 139
Requisitioning system: 115–16, 119, 122–23
Reserve components, failure to mobilize: 42, 89, 132
Revetments, construction of: 67–68
Revolutionary Development Support Directorate: 27
Rice, place in economy: 6–7
Riverine Assault Group: 73
RMK–BRJ: 25, 27, 57, 59, 61–62, 71–72, 141, 143
Roads
  benefits to South Vietnam: 112
  construction rate: 111
  construction and repair: 22, 59, 100–101, 103, 107–108, 133, 145–47
  construction standards: 45, 100–102
  controlling agencies: 100
  damage to: 99
  engineer troop force: 102, 107
  goals, by services: 111–12
  local nets: 9, 11–12, 99
  materials, procurement and shipment: 102–104
  mileage completed: 111, 122, 145
  as supply routes: 131
Rock, shortage and procurement: 102–105, 107, 109, 111
Rock drills, shortage and procurement: 104
Rubber, place in economy: 7

Sabotage: 12, 109, 130–31
Saigon: 3, 7, 9, 17, 21, 30, 37–38, 50, 52, 55, 59, 69, 72, 77, 86, 91–103, 108, 111, 143, 145
Saigon military district: 9
Saigon River and Delta: 5, 7, 59, 114
Saigon Support Command: 92
Saigon University: 102
Saigon-Hue-Hanoi railroad: 9

INDEX

Sand, stabilizing: 56–57
Sandpumper (dredge): 53–54
Schofield Barracks: 20
Seabees: 17, 27, 61, 84, 91
Secretary of the Navy: *See* Nitze, Paul H.
Seeman Board: 134
Sewage disposal
    construction program: 84–85
    construction standards: 45–46
Sharp, Admiral U. S. Grant: 16, 37, 62–63, 126–27, 129. *See also* Pacific Command.
Shell Oil Company: 124, 128, 131
Shipping
    off-loading: 50–51, 55–56
    requirements: 37
    travel time to South Vietnam: 3
Shovels, procurement: 105
Singapore: 54
Soc Trang: 126
Song Long Song: 109
Song Vam Co Tay: 9
South China Sea: 5, 53
South Pacific theater: 17
Southeast Asia theater: 17
Southeast Asia Treaty Organization (SEATO): 6
Spain: 17
Special Military Construction Study Group: 134, 138
State, Department of: 62
Storage facilities: 71, 85–87
Subic Bay: 50
Suoi Lo Maintenance and Repair Parts Activity: 100
Supply operations: 71, 85–86, 113. *See also* Logistical operations.
    accountability: 117–19
    by air: 38, 63–64
    facilities, expansion of: 69–70, 114–15
    shortages, causes of: 124
Surgical Hospital, 45th: 75
Surveys: 64

Taiwan (Formosa): 140
Tan My: 129
Tan Son Nhut: 7, 38, 69, 77, 85, 131, 143, 145
Tankers, in POL supply: 125, 128, 130
Task Force Alpha: 19
Tay Ninh: 75
Thailand: 16–17, 78, 127

Thu Bon I and *II* (dredges): 53
Thu Duc: 103, 111
Title of Authorization Act: 48
Tonkin Gulf: 5
Topography: 5
Training, deficiencies in. *See* Manpower, skilled, lack of.
Trans-Indochina Railroad: 9
Treaty of Amity and Economic Relations: 6
Tuy Hoa: 40, 62–63, 68–69, 109–10, 126, 143
Typhoons: 3, 12, 109

United States Agency for International Development (USAID): 11, 19, 23, 28, 50, 100, 109, 133, 143, 145
United States Air Force (USAF): 16–19, 21, 26, 29–30, 46, 62–63, 65, 68, 80, 84, 86–87, 90–91, 125–27, 141. *See also* Air Force, Seventh.
United States Army, Pacific (USARPAC): 30–31, 138
United States Army, Ryukyu Islands (USARYIS): 40
United States Army, Vietnam (USARV). *See also* United States Army Support Group, Vietnam.
    activation: 16
    engineer staff: 24–25
    move to Long Binh: 77
    troop strength: 6, 14, 19–20
United States Army Base Development Board: 138
United States Army commitments: 6, 15, 19–20
United States Army Construction Agency, Vietnam: 31, 34
United States Army Engineer Command, Vietnam: 24, 27, 43, 73, 122, 141
United States Army Engineer Construction Agency, Vietnam: 24, 30, 92–93, 97, 103, 114
United States Army Engineer Hydrographic Survey: 107
United States Army Facilities Components System: 138
United States Army Headquarters Area Command: 30, 92
United States Army Materiel Command: 117

United States Army Procurement Agency, Vietnam: 92–93
United States Army Support Command, Vietnam: 30
United States Army Support Group, Vietnam: 13, 15–16. *See also* United States Army, Vietnam.
United States Construction Staff Committee: 17
United States Continental Army Command: 21
United States Embassy: 27–29, 35, 108–109
United States Marine Corps: 17, 19, 46, 61, 68–69, 86, 125. *See also* Marine Amphibious Force, III; Marine Divisions; Marine Regiments.
United States Military Assistance Command, Vietnam. *See also* Harkins, General Paul D.; Westmoreland, General William C.
  activation: 13
  command and staff structure: 13–16, 19
  engineer staff: 29–30, 40–41
  headquarters construction: 145
  Republic of Vietnam Armed Forces, relationship with: 16
  supply system: 114
United States Navy: 16–19, 21, 25–26, 29, 46–47, 52, 62–63, 68–69, 73, 83–84, 91, 93, 115, 117, 125–27, 129, 133, 141, 143. *See also subordinate agencies by name.*

Vance, Cyrus R.: 63
Viet Cong: 109
Vietnam armed forces. *See* Republic of Vietnam Armed Forces.
Vietnam Railway System: 108–109
Vin Long: 125
Vinnell Corporation: 27, 78–81, 90
Vu-Graph: 115
Vung Ro: 40, 54, 143
Vung Ro Bay: 126
Vung Tau: 19, 30, 38, 52–55, 59, 69, 73, 75, 79–80, 102, 107, 117, 126, 143

Water supply
  construction program: 11, 83–84, 143–45, 147
  construction standards: 45–46
Water table, local: 85
Weather: 3, 11–12
Well-drilling: 11, 83–84, 143–45
Werth, Captain Maury, U.S. Navy: 59
West, local contact with: 6
Westmoreland, General William C.: 14, 16–17, 30, 37, 45–46, 48–49, 62, 74, 77, 87, 103, 108, 142. *See also* United States Army, Vietnam; United States Military Assistance Command, Vietnam.
Wilbur, Lyman D.: 25
Women, training of: 141

Xuan Loc: 111

www.ingramcontent.com/pod-product-compliance
Lightning Source LLC
Chambersburg PA
CBHW030141170426
43199CB00008B/152